FOR ORGANS, PIANOS & ELECTRONIC KEYBOARDS

E-Z PLAY® TODAY

164

❄ THE BEST ❄
CHRISTMAS
SONGBOOK

3rd Edition

ISBN 978-1-5400-2912-6

Hal•Leonard®

E-Z Play® Today Music Notation © 1975 by HAL LEONARD LLC
E-Z PLAY and EASY ELECTRONIC KEYBOARD MUSIC are registered trademarks of HAL LEONARD LLC.

Visit Hal Leonard Online at
www.halleonard.com

Contact Us:
Hal Leonard
7777 West Bluemound Road
Milwaukee, WI 53213
Email: info@halleonard.com

In Europe contact:
Hal Leonard Europe Limited
Distribution Centre, Newmarket Road
Bury St Edmunds, Suffolk, IP33 3YB
Email: info@halleonardeurope.com

In Australia contact:
Hal Leonard Australia Pty. Ltd.
4 Lentara Court
Cheltenham, Victoria, 3192 Australia
Email: info@halleonard.com.au

Auld Lang Syne

Registration 2
Rhythm: None

Words by Robert Burns
Traditional Scottish Melody

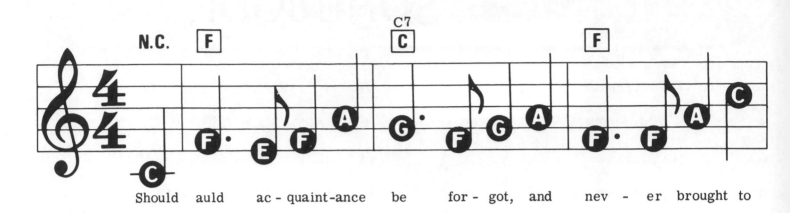

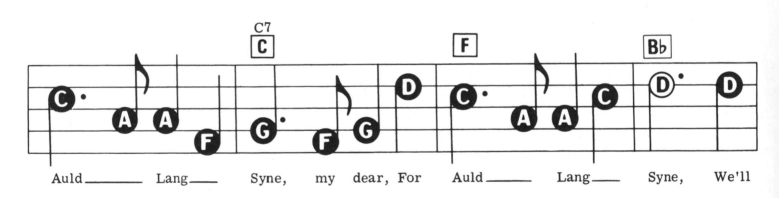

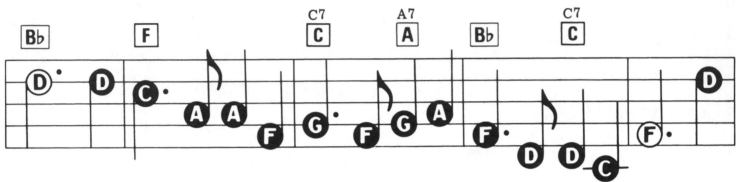

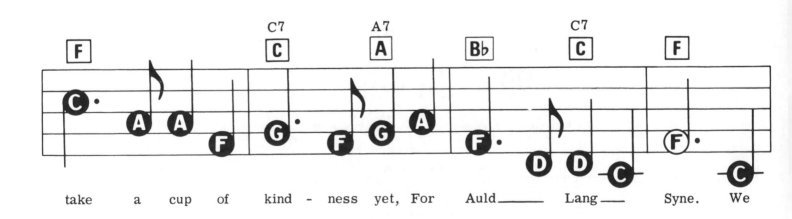

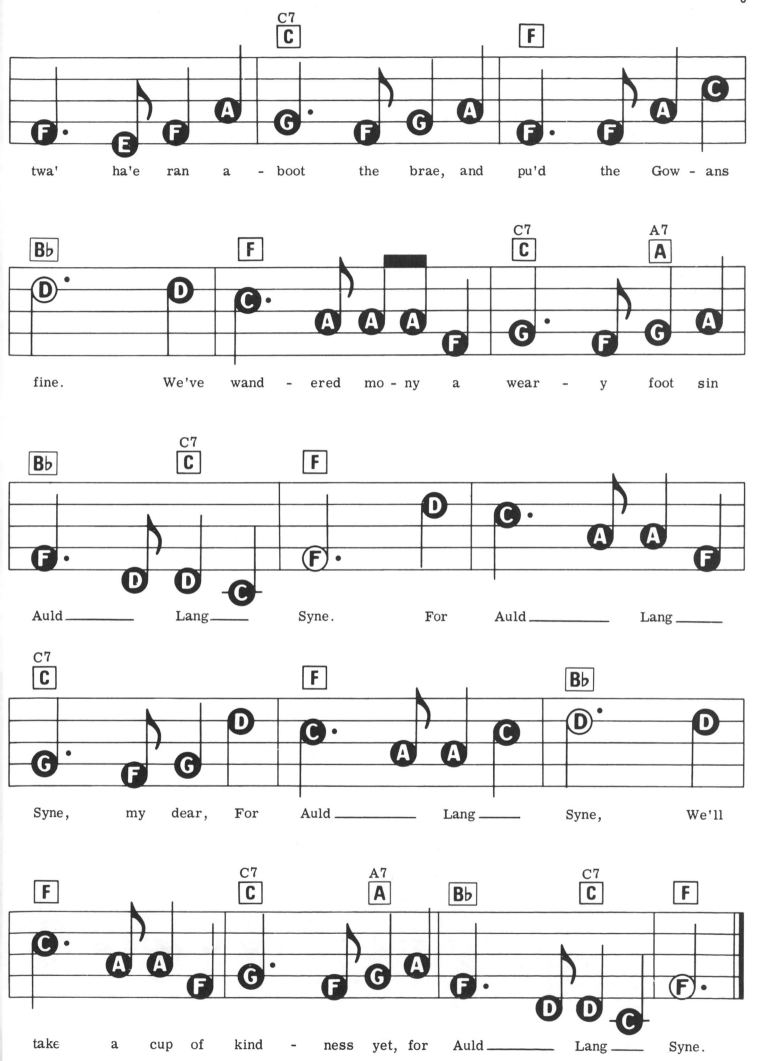

Away in a Manger

Registration 1
Rhythm: Waltz

Traditional
Words by John T. McFarland (v.3)
Music by William J. Kirkpatrick

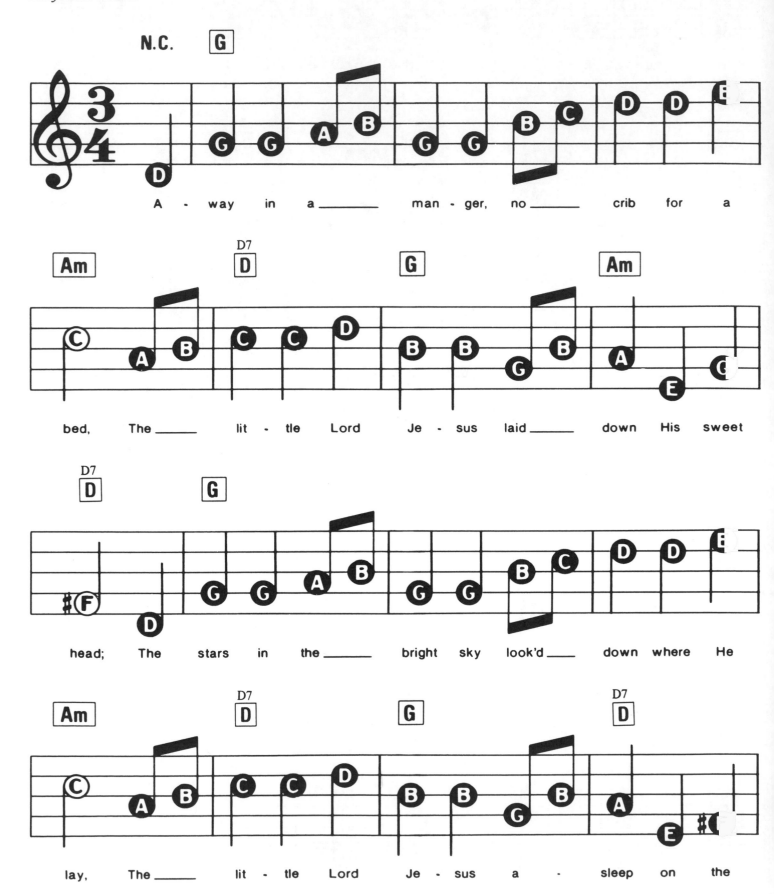

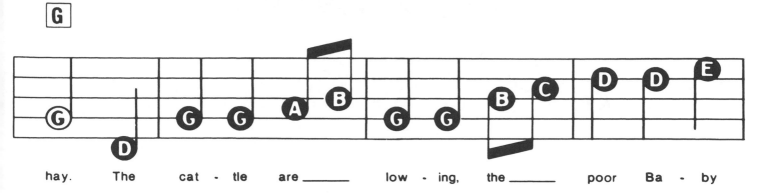

hay. The cat - tle are _____ low - ing, the _____ poor Ba - by

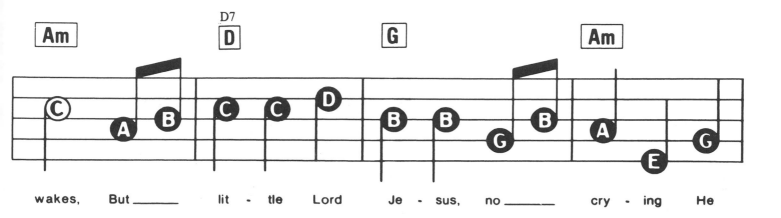

wakes, But _____ lit - tle Lord Je - sus, no _____ cry - ing He

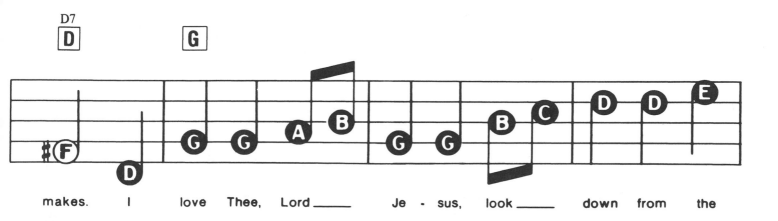

makes. I love Thee, Lord _____ Je - sus, look _____ down from the

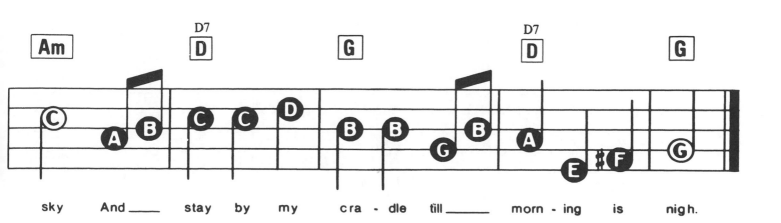

sky And _____ stay by my cra - dle till _____ morn - ing is nigh.

Blue Christmas

Registration 3
Rhythm: Fox Trot or Swing

Words and Music by Billy Hayes
and Jay Johnson

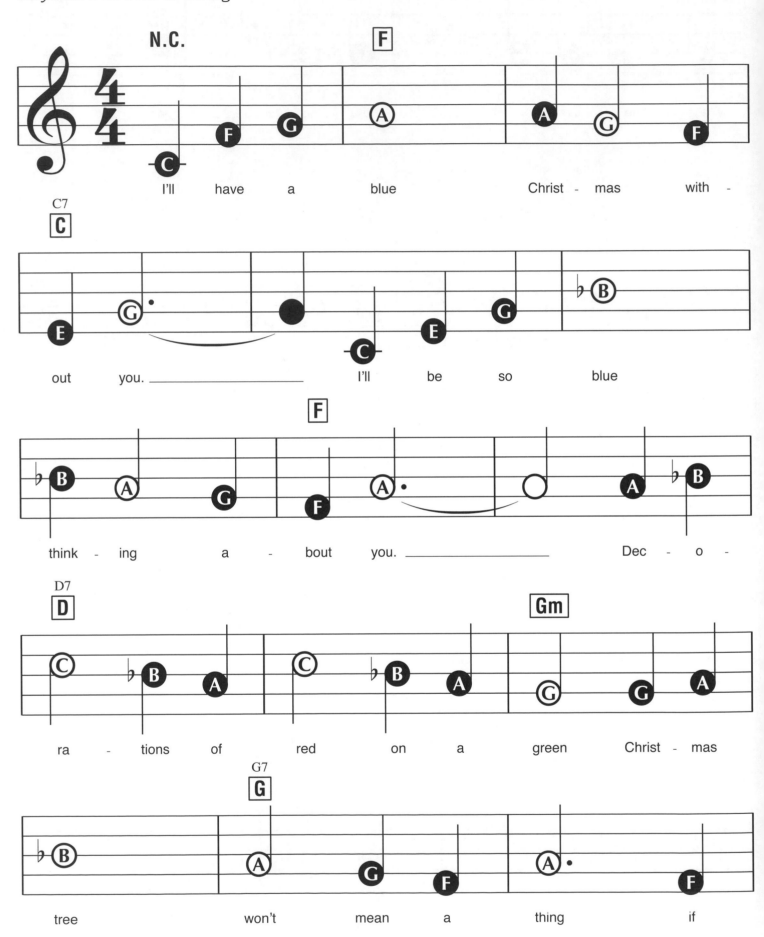

7

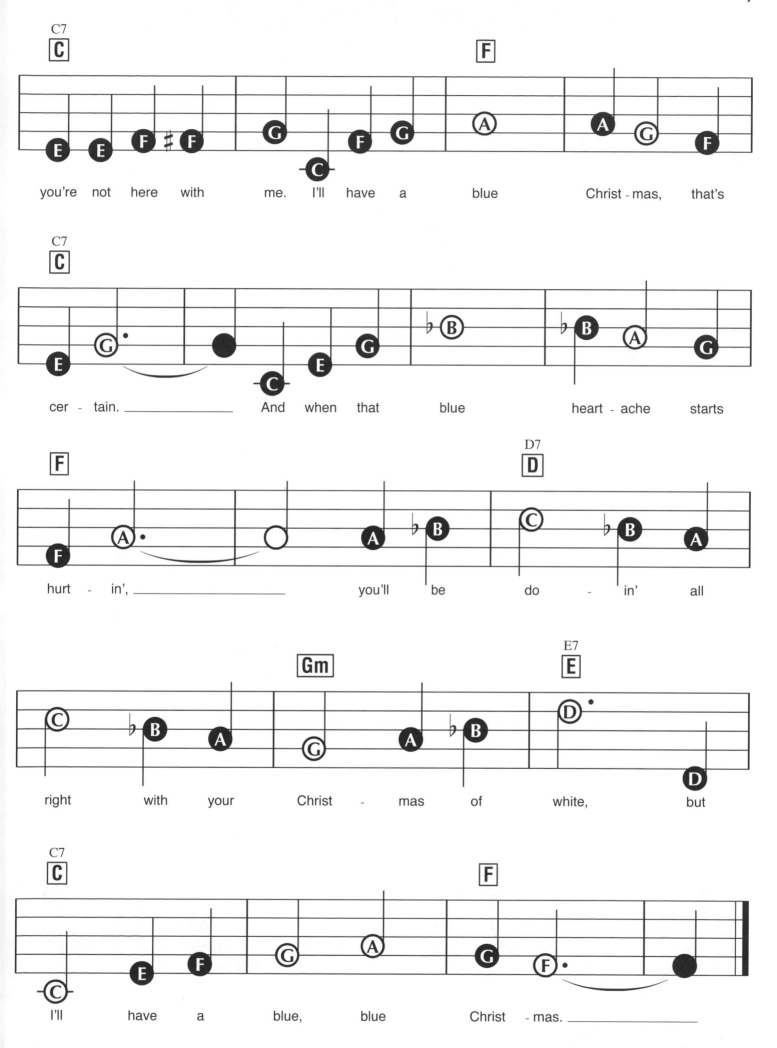

Christmas Time Is Here
from A CHARLIE BROWN CHRISTMAS

Registration 8
Rhythm: Waltz

Words by Lee Mendelson
Music by Vince Guaraldi

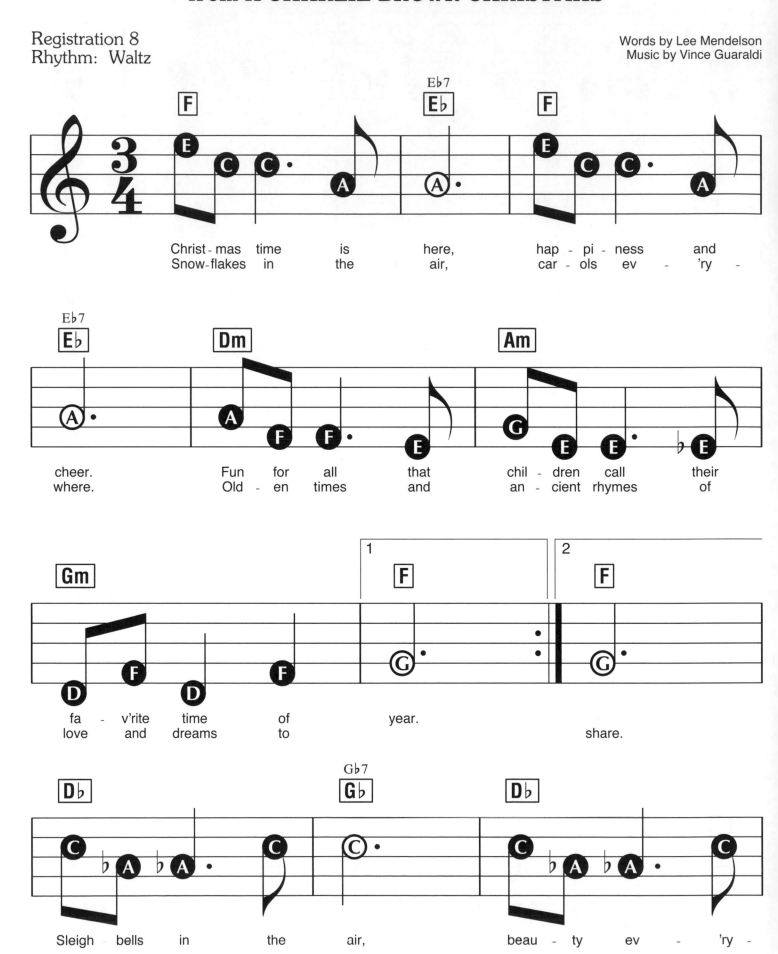

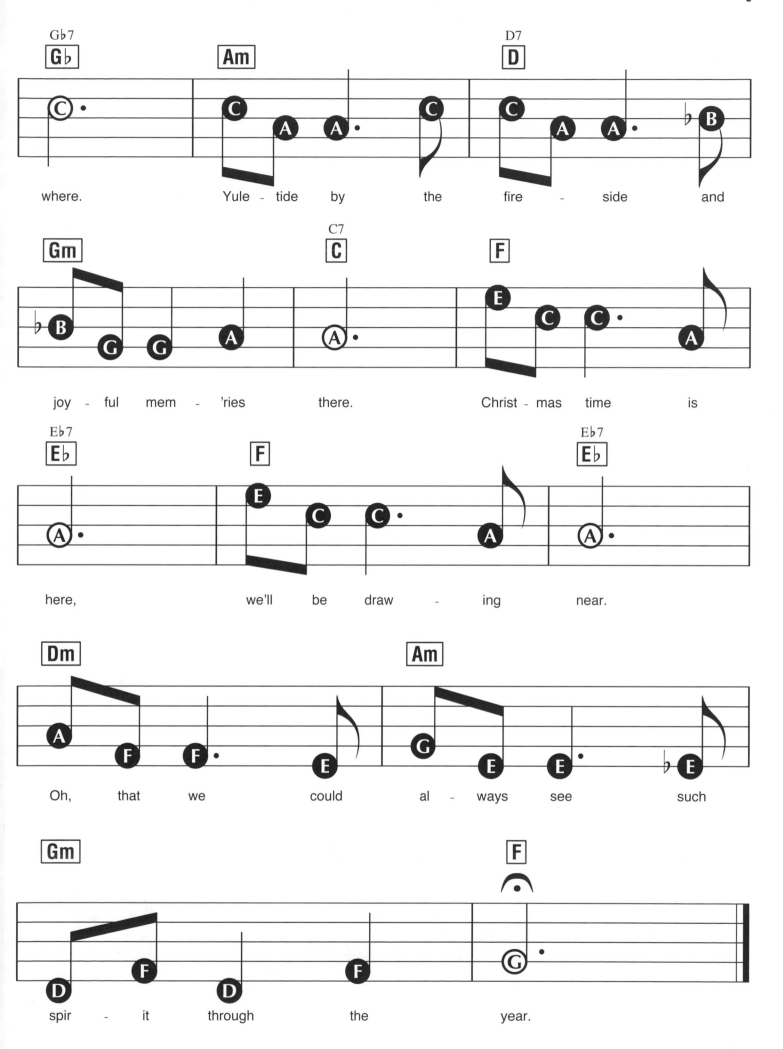

Deck the Hall

Registration 7
Rhythm: Fox Trot

Traditional Welsh Carol

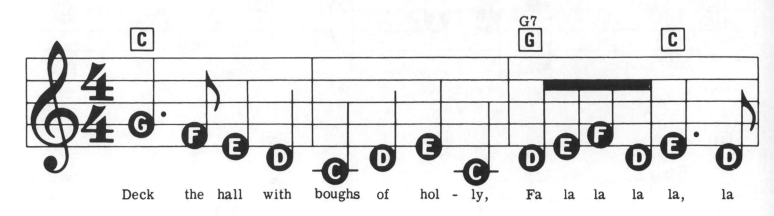

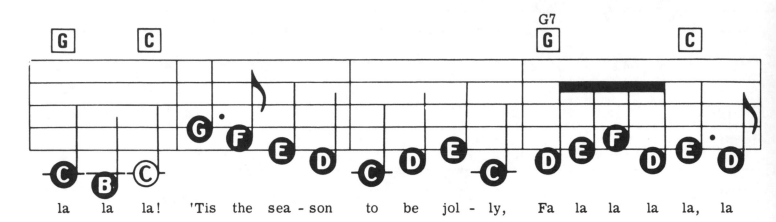

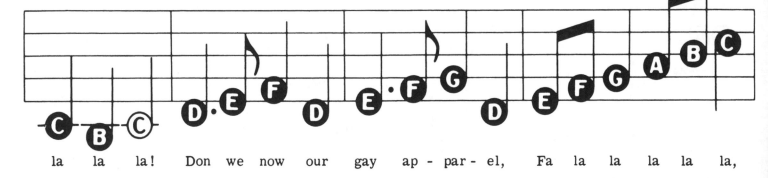

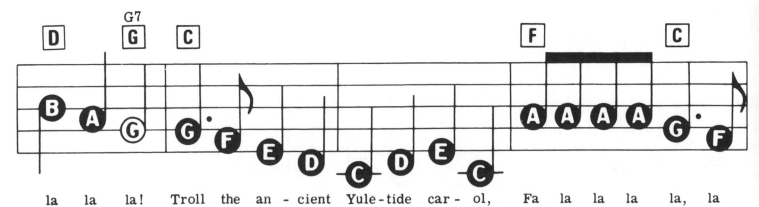

11

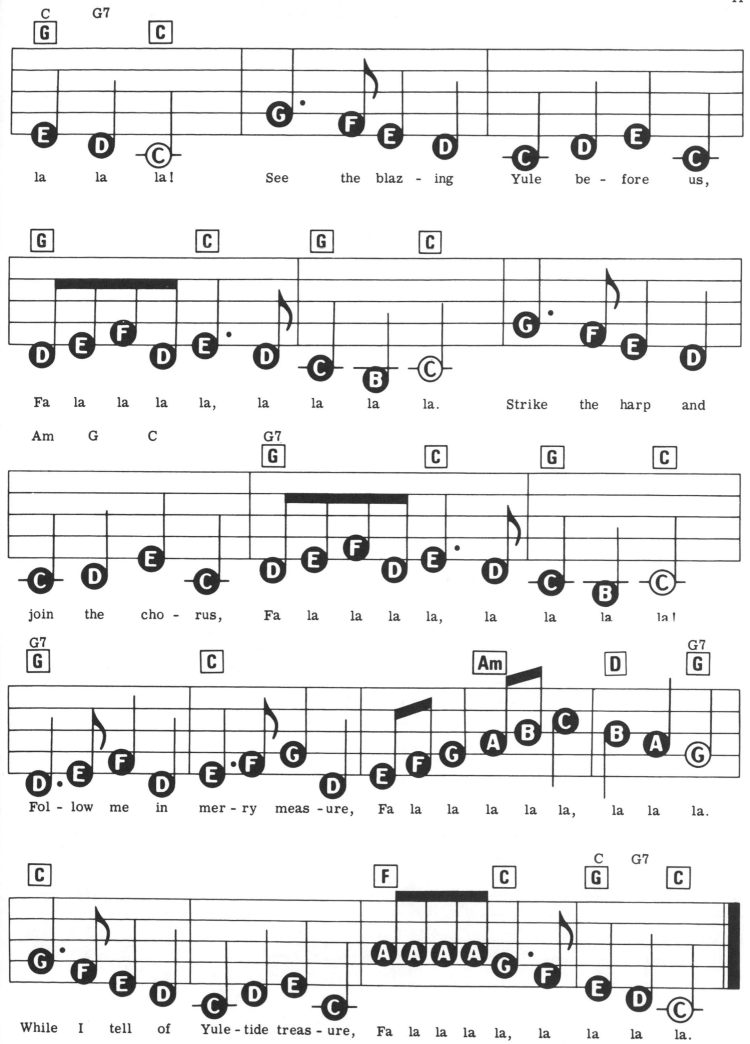

Do You Hear What I Hear

Registration 4
Rhythm: 8-Beat or Pops

Words and Music by Noel Regney
and Gloria Shayne

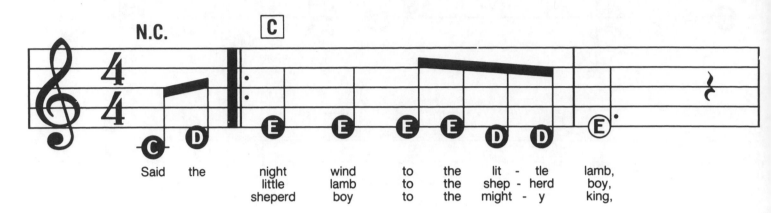

Said the night wind to the lit - tle lamb,
little lamb to the shep - herd boy,
sheperd boy to the might - y king,

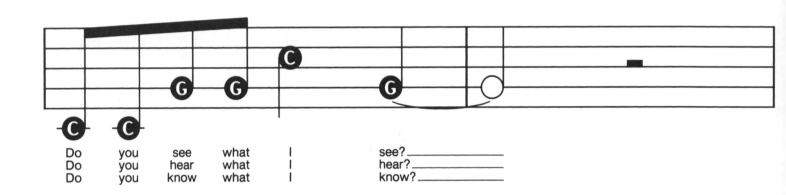

Do you see what I see?
Do you hear what I hear?
Do you know what I know?

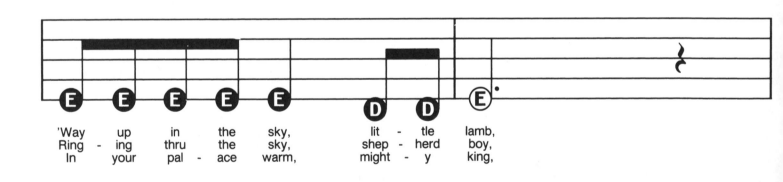

'Way up in the sky, lit - tle lamb,
Ring - ing thru the sky, shep - herd boy,
In your pal - ace warm, might - y king,

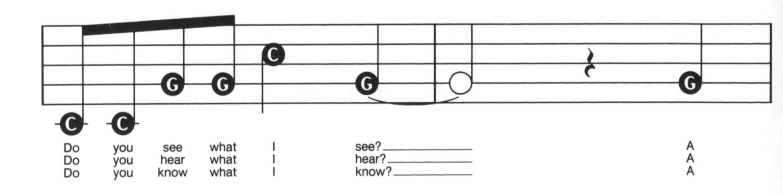

Do you see what I see?
Do you hear what I hear?
Do you know what I know?

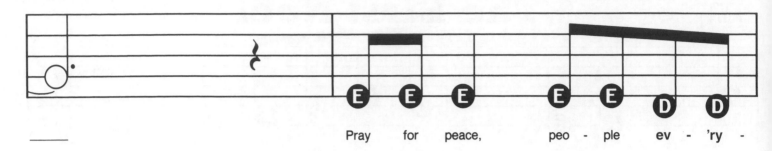

_____ Pray for peace, peo - ple ev - 'ry -

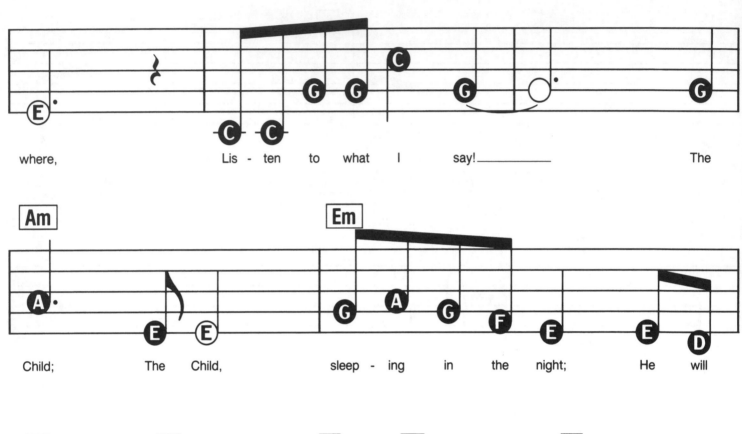

where, Lis - ten to what I say!_____ The

Am   **Em**

Child; The Child, sleep - ing in the night; He will

F   **G**   **E**   **G**   **F**

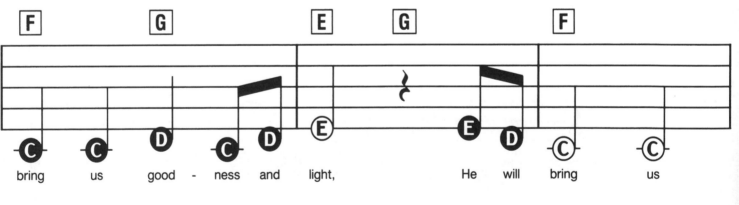

bring us good - ness and light, He will bring us

G7

G   **C**

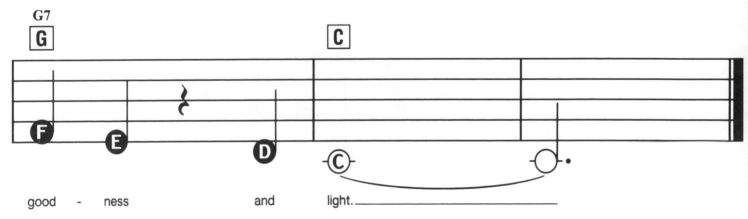

good - ness and light._____

The First Noël

Registration 6
Rhythm: None

17th Century English Carol
Music from W. Sandys' *Christmas Carols*

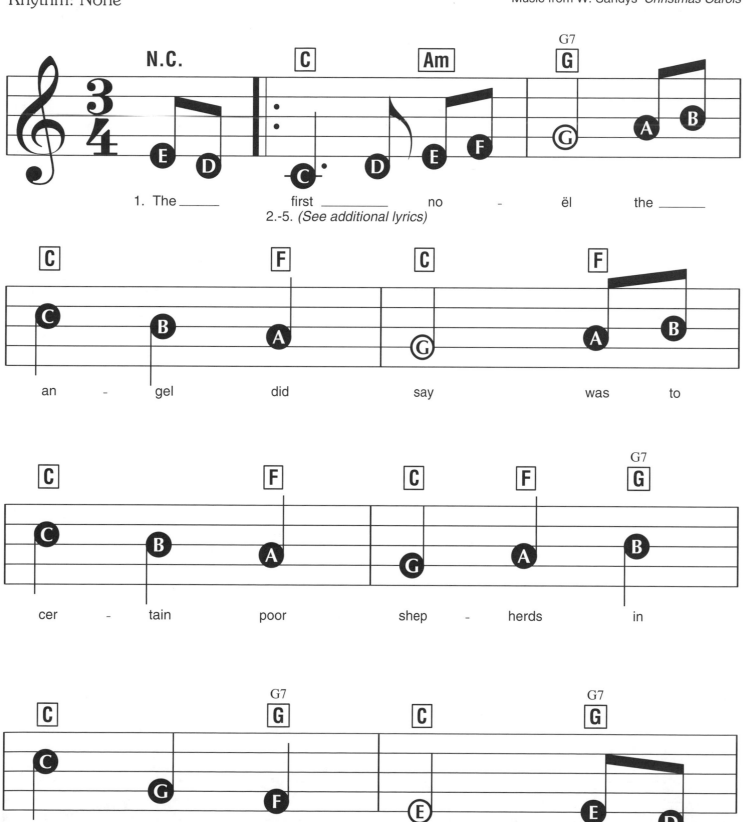

1. The _____ first _____ no - ël the _____
2.-5. *(See additional lyrics)*

an - gel did say was to

cer - tain poor shep - herds in

fields as they lay. In _____

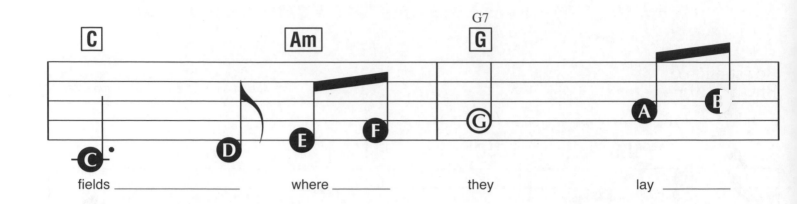

fields _____ where _____ they lay _____

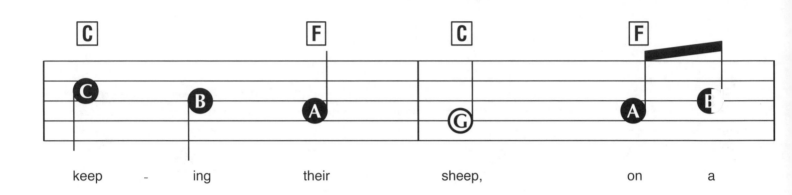

keep - ing their sheep, on a

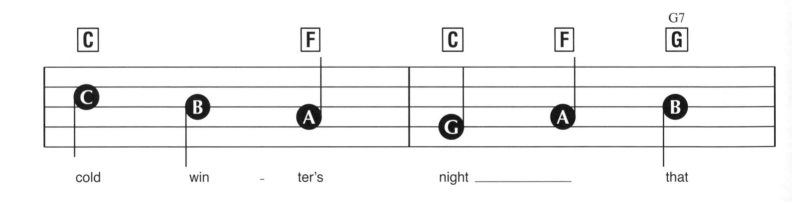

cold win - ter's night _____ that

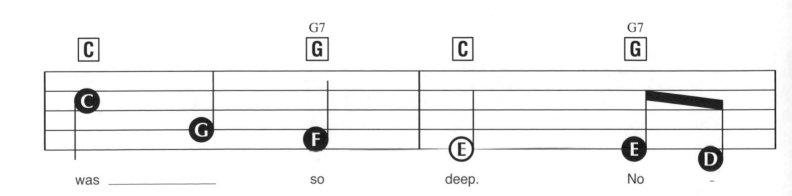

was _____ so deep. No -

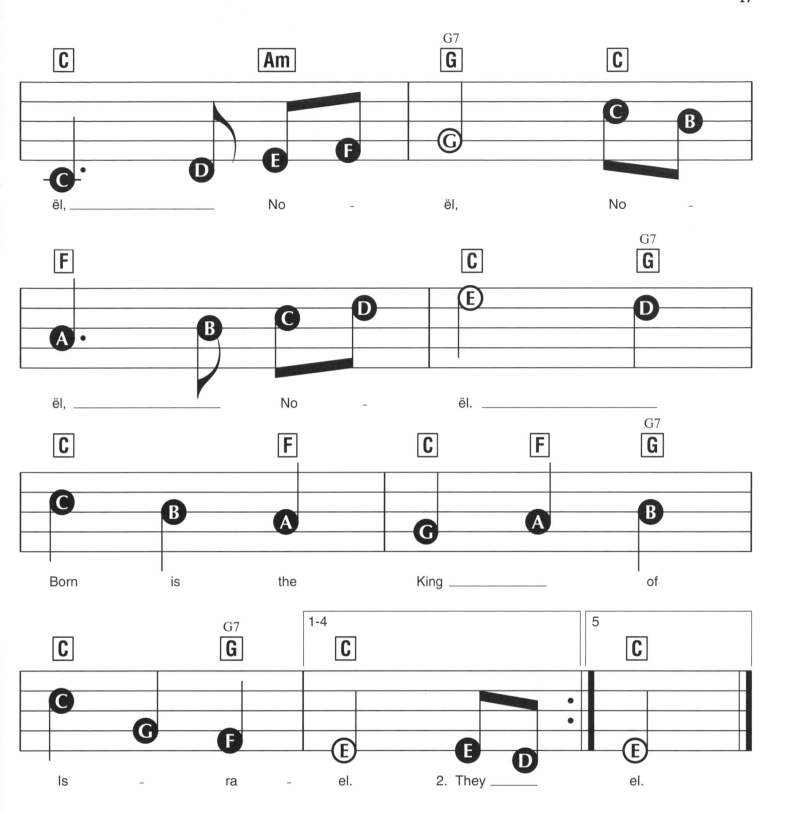

Additional Lyrics

2. They looked up and saw a star
   Shining in the east beyond them far.
   And to the earth it gave great light,
   And so it continued both day and night.
   Noël, Noël, Noël, Noël.
   Born is the King of Israel.

3. And by the light of that same star
   Three wise men came from country far.
   To seek for a King was their intent,
   And to follow the star wherever it went.
   Noël, Noël, Noël, Noël.
   Born is the King of Israel.

4. This star drew nigh to the northwest,
   O'er Bethlehem it took its rest.
   And there it did both stop and stay
   Right over the place where Jesus lay.
   Noël, Noël, Noël, Noël.
   Born is the King of Israel.

5. Then entered in those wise men three
   Full reverently upon their knee.
   And offered there, in His presence,
   Their gold, and myrrh, and frankincense.
   Noël, Noël, Noël, Noël.
   Born is the King of Israel.

Frosty the Snow Man

Registration 2
Rhythm: Fox Trot or Swing

Words and Music by Steve Nelson
and Jack Rollins

19

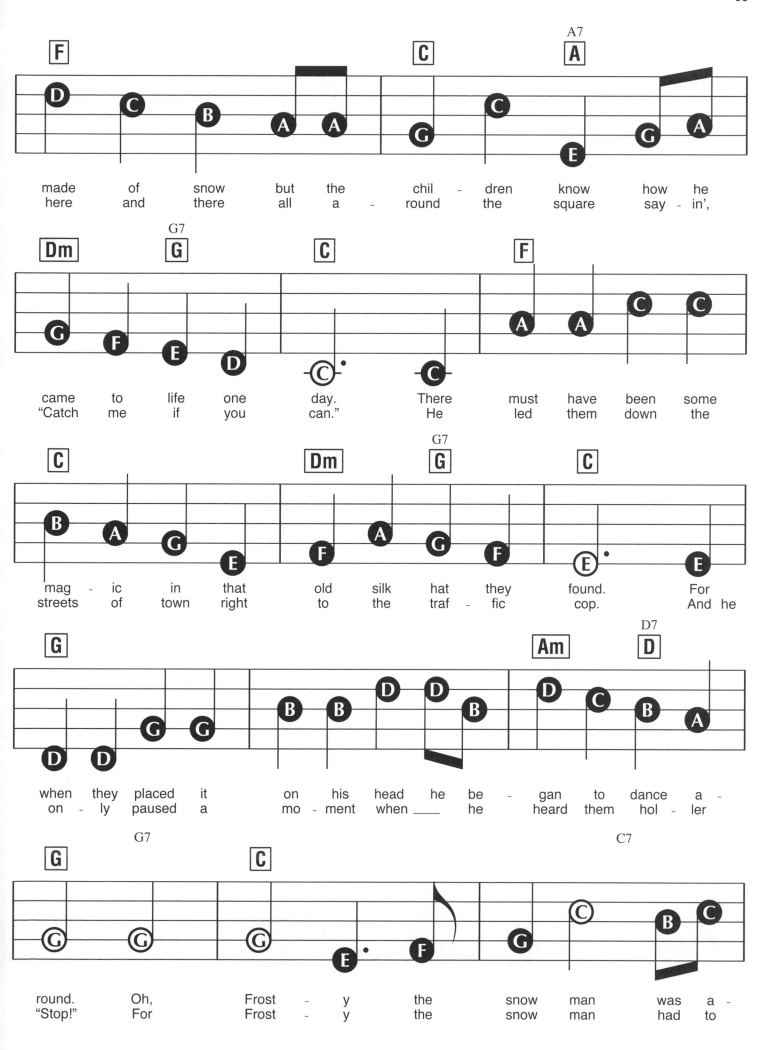

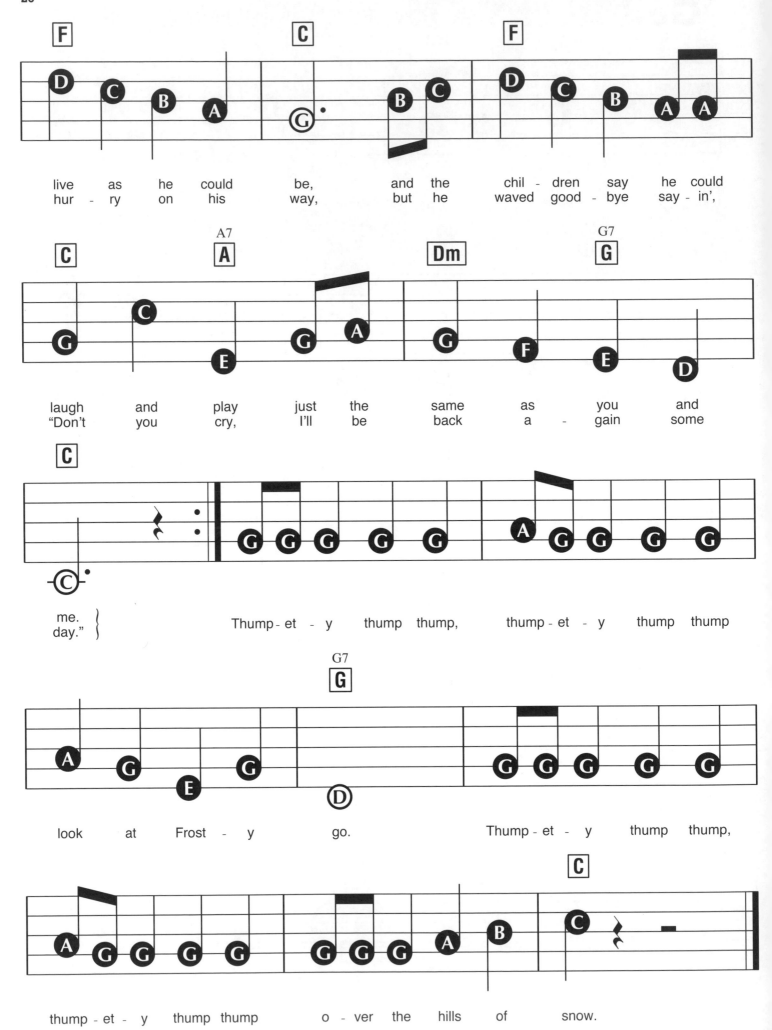

God Rest Ye Merry, Gentlemen

Registration 6
Rhythm: None

19th Century English Carol

God rest ye mer - ry, gen - tle - men, let
God, our heav - 'nly Fa - ther, a

noth - ing you dis - may. Re - mem - ber Christ our
bless - ed an - gel came, and un - to cer - tain

Sav - ior was brought born on Christ - mas Day, to
shep - herds brought tid - ings of the same; how

save us all from Sa - tan's pow'r when we were gone a -
that in Beth - le - hem was born the Son of God by

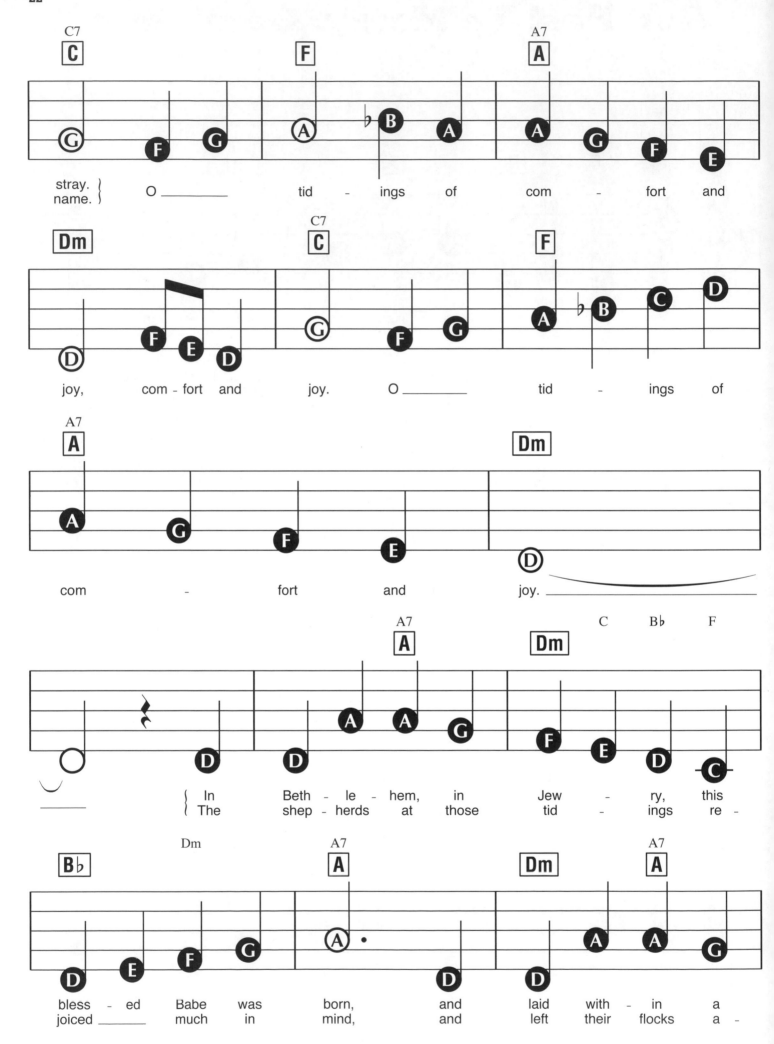

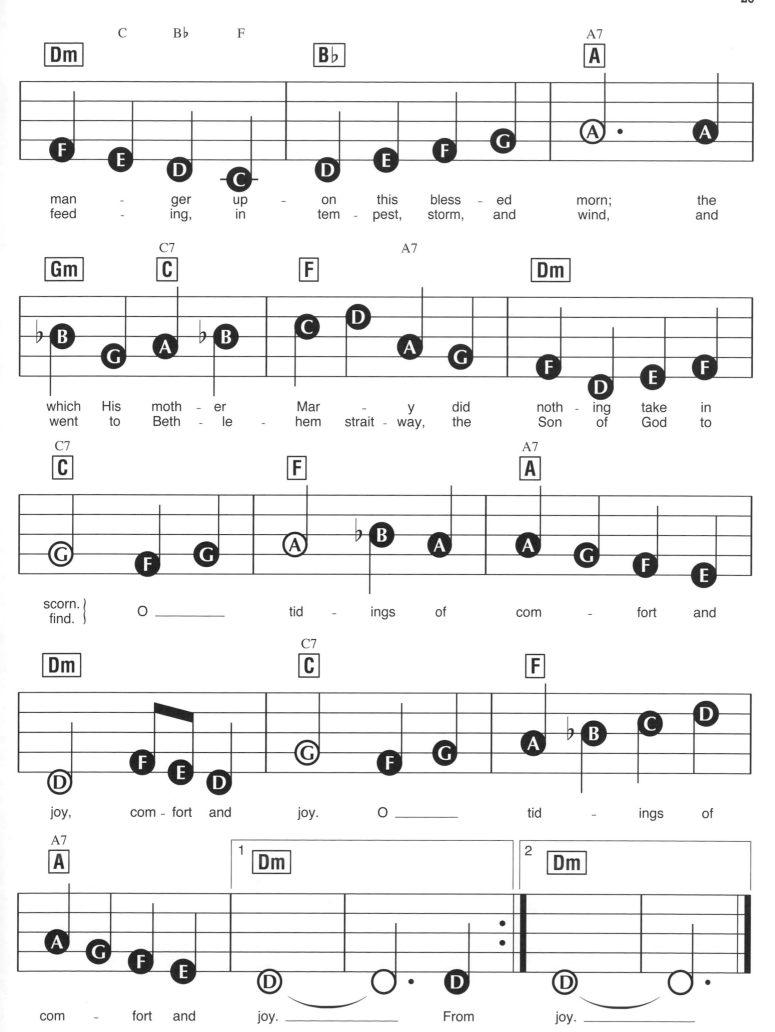

Hark! The Herald Angels Sing

Words by Charles Wesley
Music by Felix Mendelssohn-Bartholdy
Adapted by William H. Cummings

Registration 6
Rhythm: None

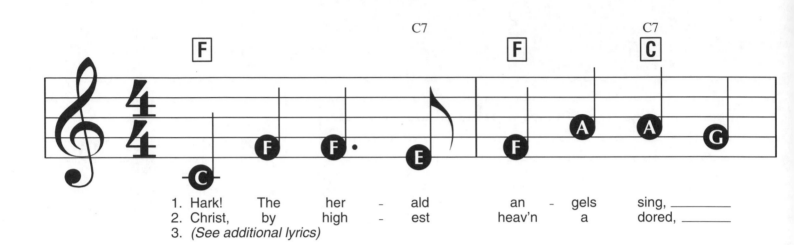

1. Hark! The her - ald an - gels sing, _____
2. Christ, by high - est heav'n a - dored, _____
3. *(See additional lyrics)*

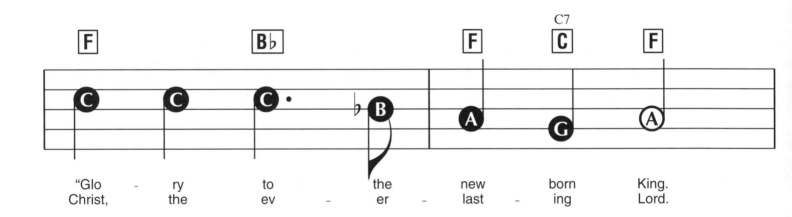

"Glo - ry to the new born King.
Christ, the ev - er - last - ing Lord.

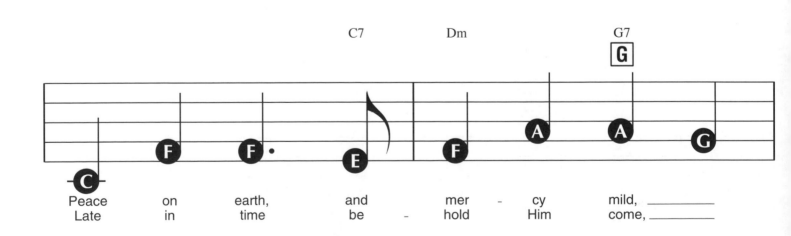

Peace on earth, and mer - cy mild, _____
Late in time be - hold Him come, _____

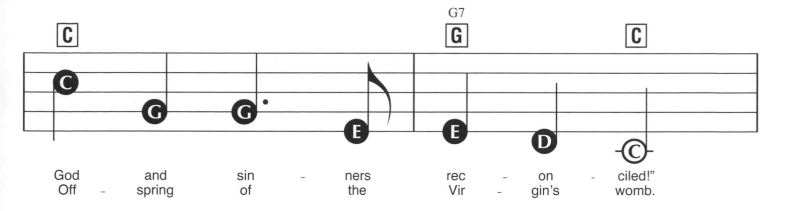

God   and   sin -   ners   rec - on - ciled!"
Off - spring   of   the   Vir - gin's   womb.

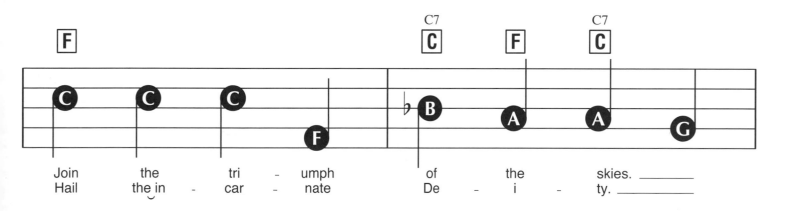

Joy - ful,   all   ye   na - tions, rise, _____
Veiled   in   flesh   the   God - head see; _____

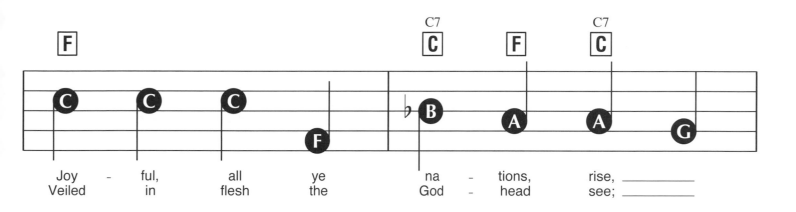

Join   the   tri - umph   of   the   skies. _____
Hail   the in - car - nate   De - i - ty. _____

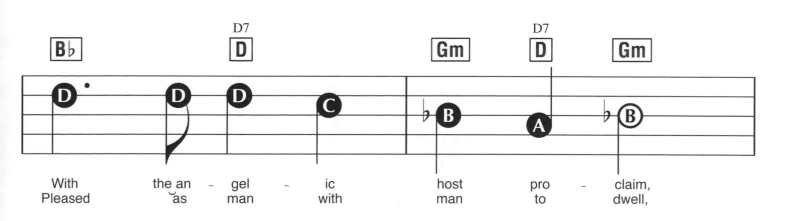

With   the an - gel - ic   host   pro - claim,
Pleased   as man   with   man   to   dwell,

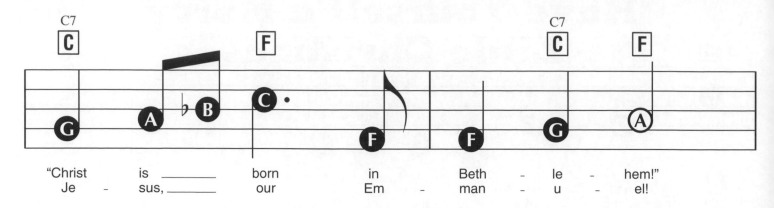

"Christ   is _____ born   in   Beth - le - hem!"
Je - sus, _____ our   Em - man - u - el!

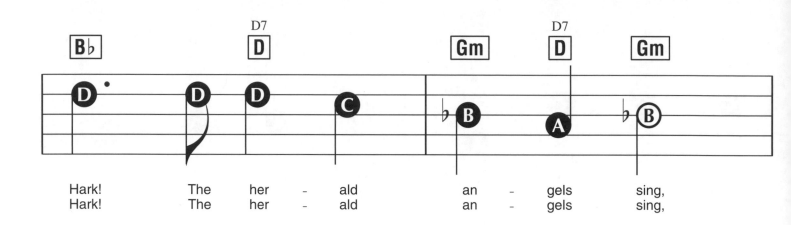

Hark!   The   her - ald   an - gels   sing,
Hark!   The   her - ald   an - gels   sing,

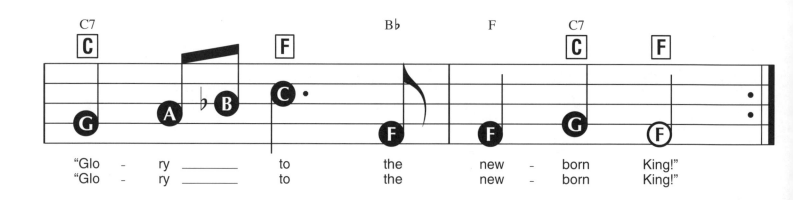

"Glo - ry _____ to   the   new - born   King!"
"Glo - ry _____ to   the   new - born   King!"

Additional Lyrics

3. Hail the heaven-born Prince of Peace!
   Hail the Sun of Righteousness!
   Light and life to all he brings,
   Risen with healing in His wings.
   Mild He lays His glory by,
   Born that man no more may die.
   Born to raise the sons of earth,
   Born to give them second birth.

   Hark! the herald angels sing,
   "Glory to the newborn King!"

Have Yourself a Merry Little Christmas

from MEET ME IN ST. LOUIS

Registration 1
Rhythm: Fox Trot or Ballad

Words and Music by Hugh Martin
and Ralph Blane

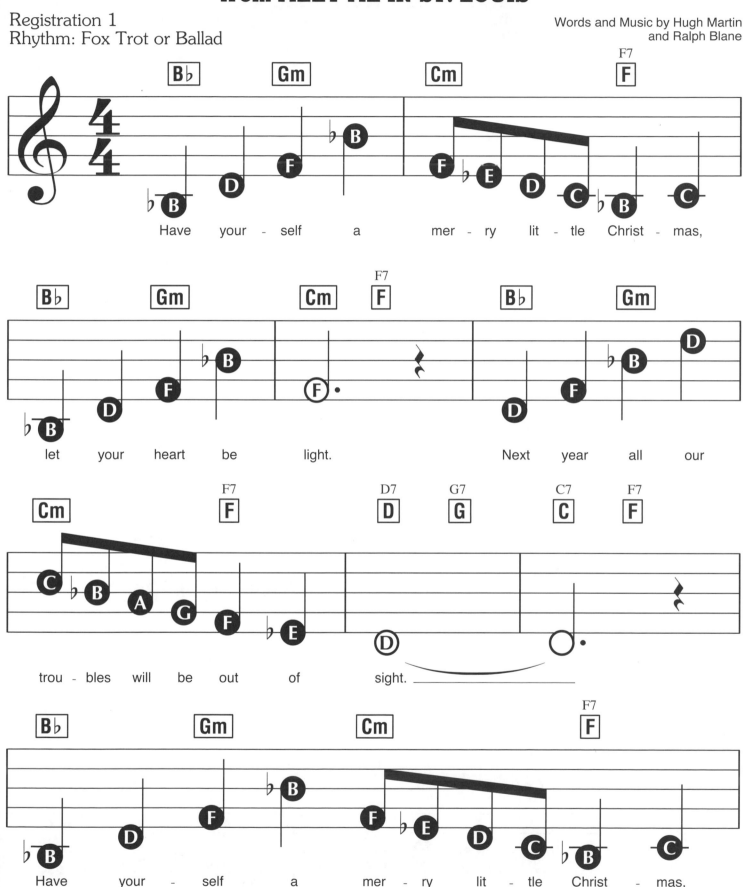

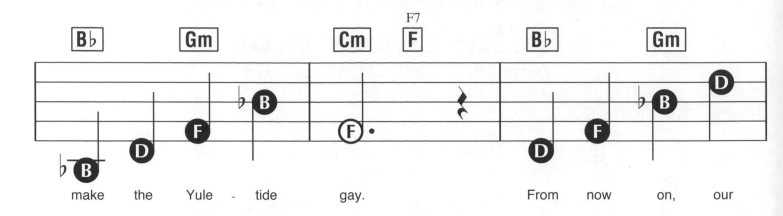

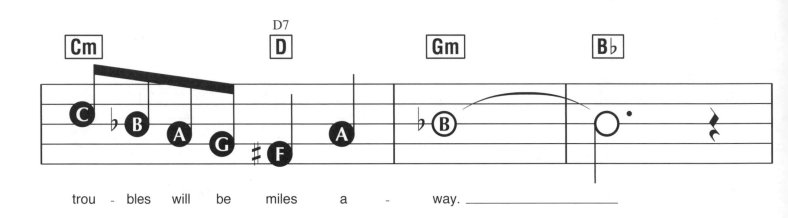

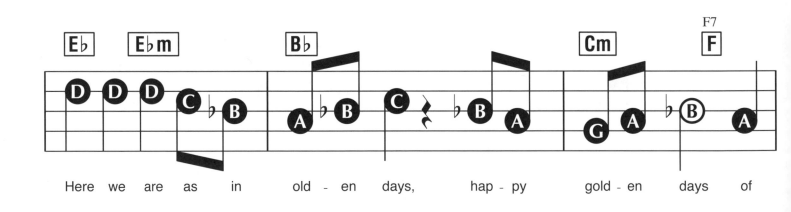

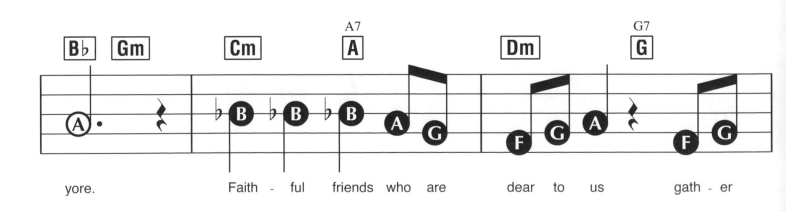

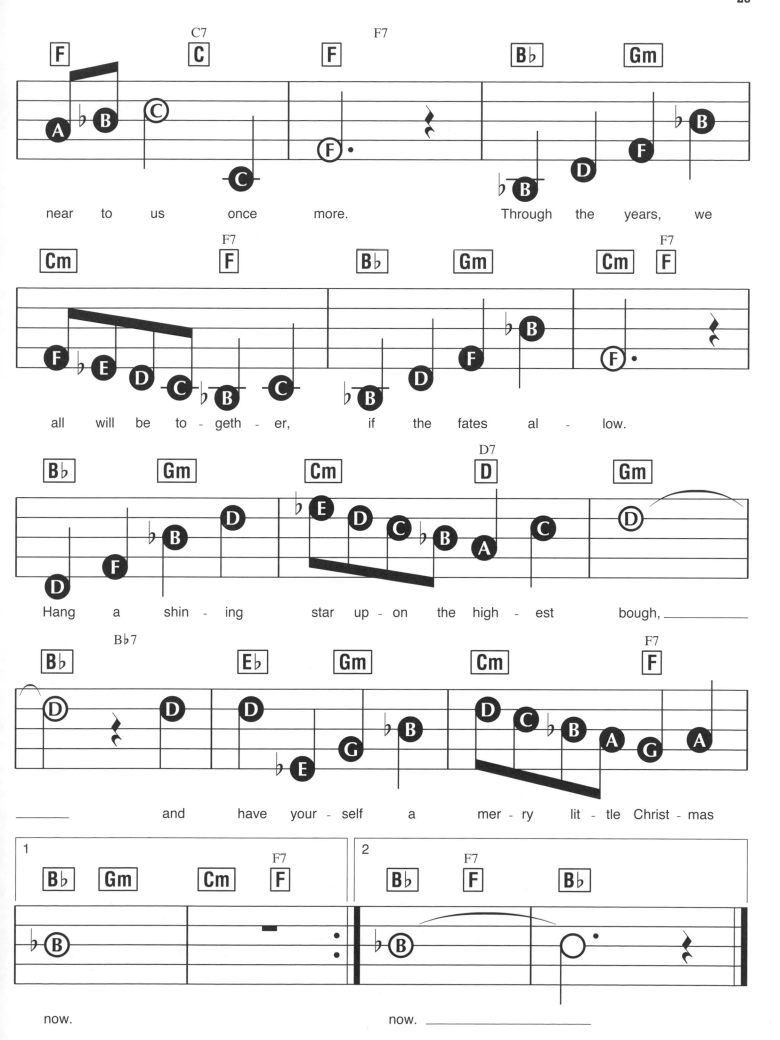

Here Comes Santa Claus
(Right Down Santa Claus Lane)

Registration 4
Rhythm: Swing

Words and Music by Gene Autry
and Oakley Halderman

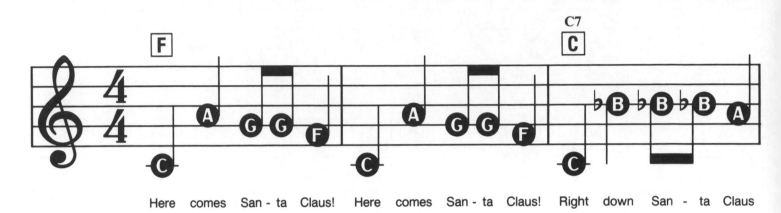

Here comes San - ta Claus! Here comes San - ta Claus! Right down San - ta Claus

Lane!

1. Vix - en and Blitz - en and all his rein - deer are
2. He's got a bag that is all filled with toys for the

pull - ing on the rein. Bells are ring - ing,
boys and girls a - gain. Hear those sleigh - bells

chil - dren sing - ing, all is mer - ry and bright.
jin - gle jan - gle, what a beau - ti - ful sight.

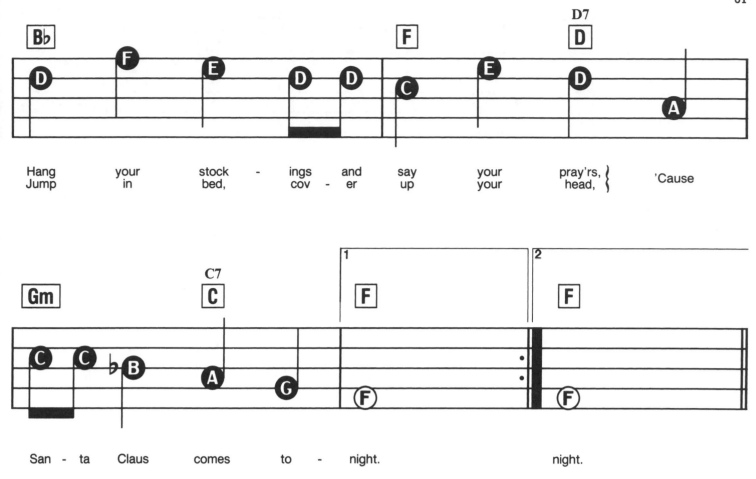

Hang your stock - ings and say your pray'rs,
Jump in bed, cov - er up your head,
'Cause

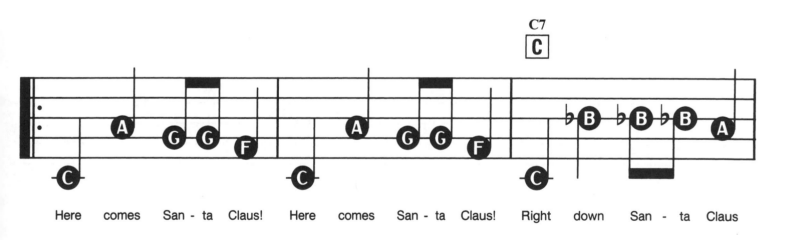

San - ta Claus comes to - night.
night.

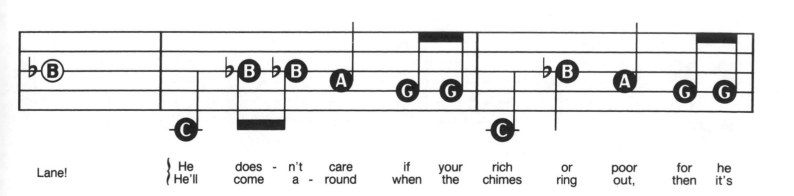

Here comes San - ta Claus! Here comes San - ta Claus! Right down San - ta Claus

Lane!
He does - n't care if your rich or poor, for he
He'll come a - round when the chimes ring out, then it's

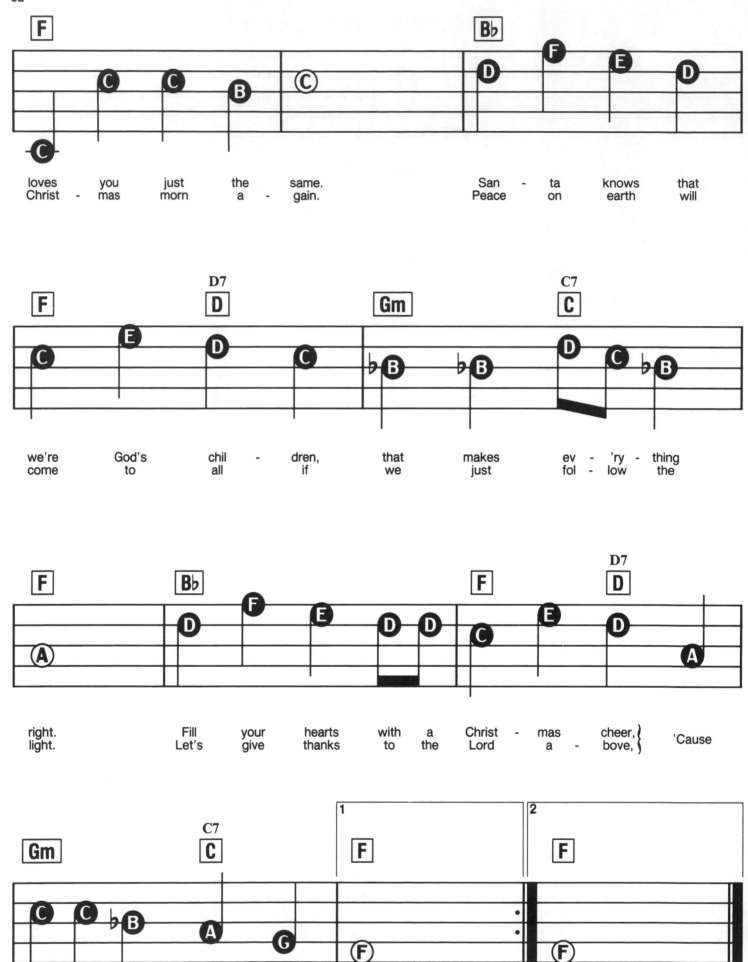

loves you just the same. San - ta knows that
Christ - mas morn a - gain. Peace on earth that will

we're God's chil - dren, that makes ev - 'ry - thing
come to all if we just fol - low the

right. Fill your hearts with a Christ - mas cheer,} 'Cause
light. Let's give thanks to the Lord a - bove,}

San - ta Claus comes to - night. night.

Let It Snow!
Let It Snow! Let It Snow!

Registration 7
Rhythm: Fox Trot or Swing

Words by Sammy Cahn
Music by Jule Styne

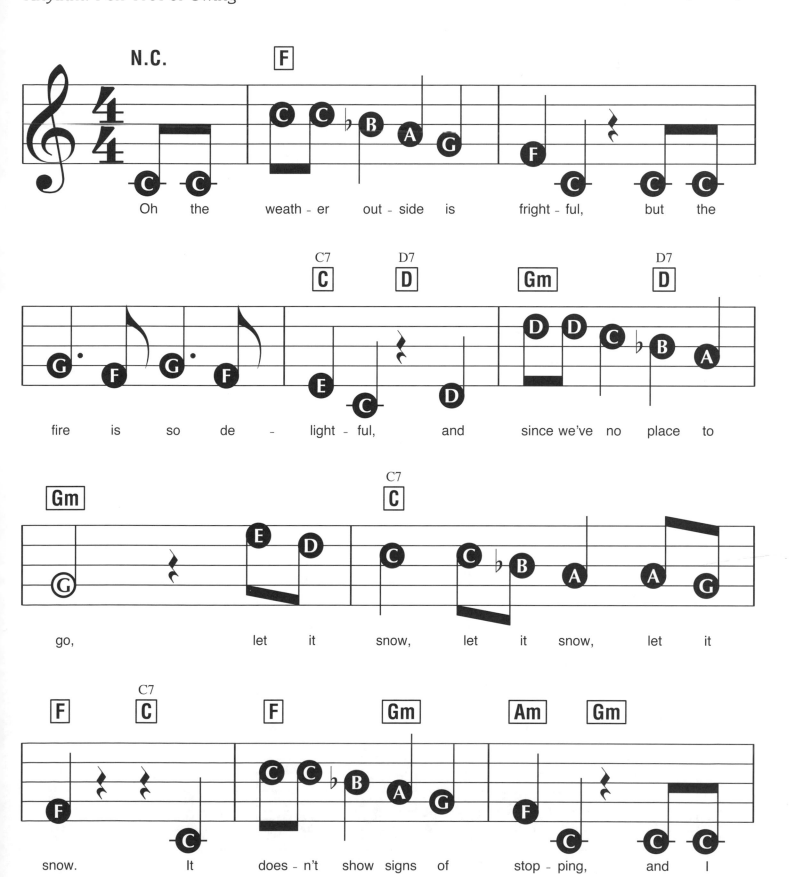

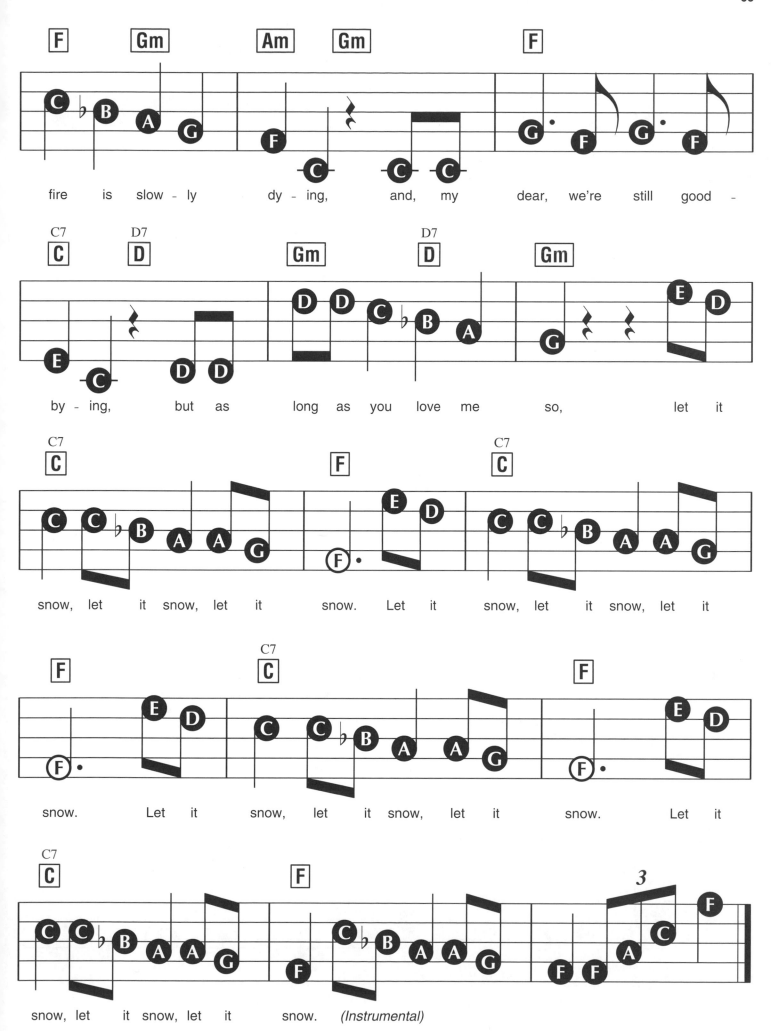

I Heard the Bells on Christmas Day

Registration 9
Rhythm: Ballad

Words by Henry Wadsworth Longfellow
Adapted by Johnny Marks
Music by Johnny Marks

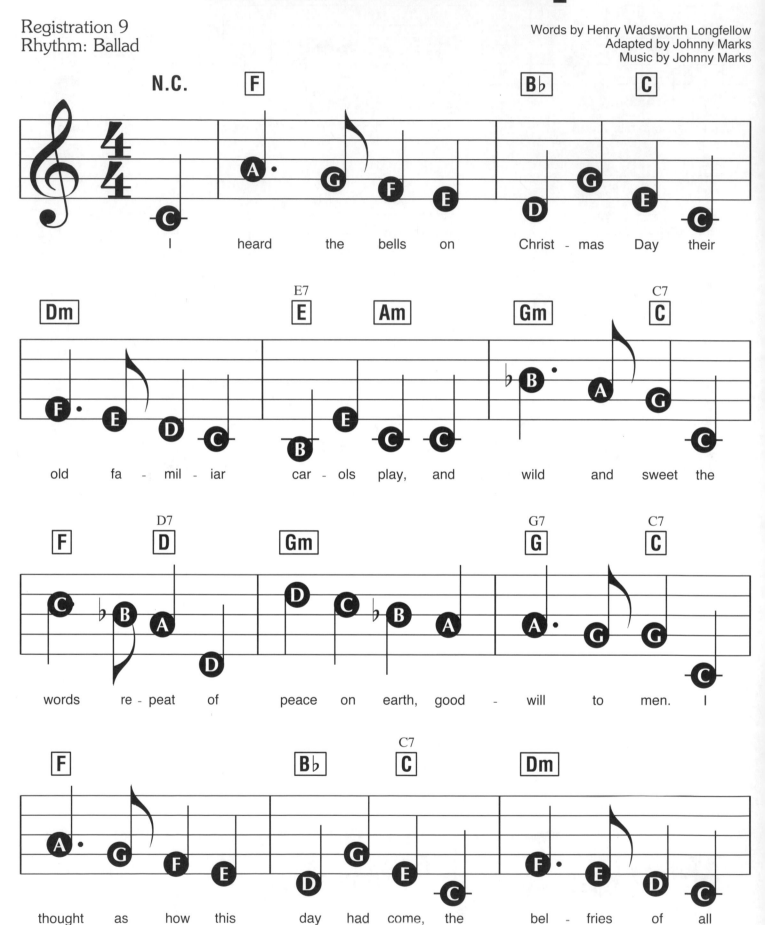

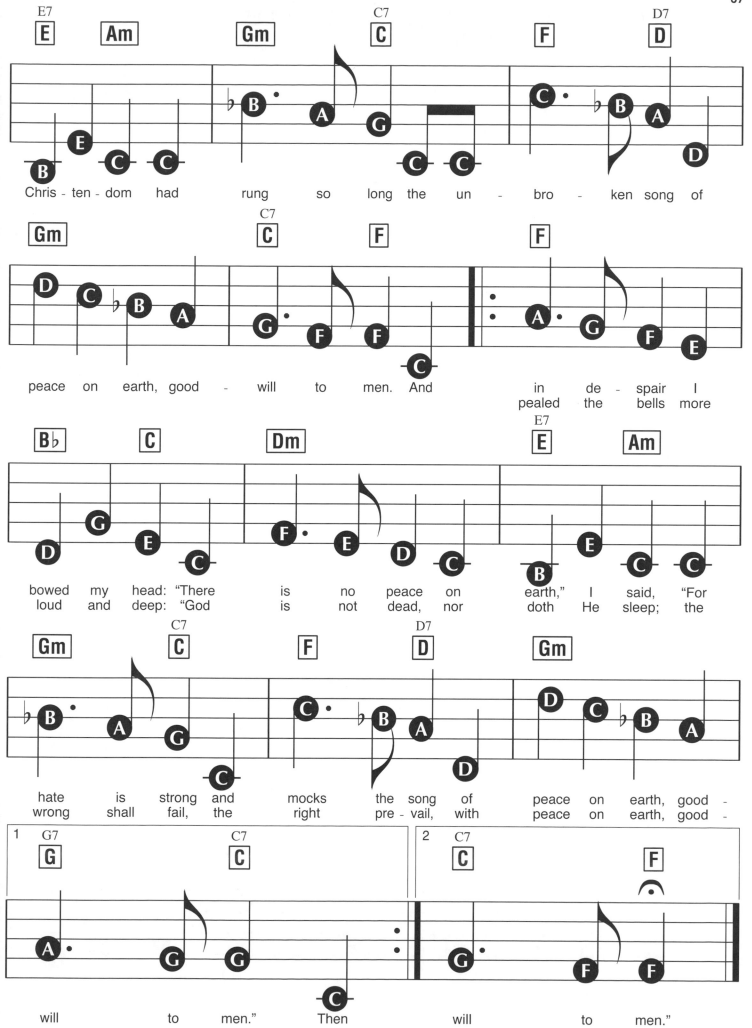

I'll Be Home for Christmas

Registration 1
Rhythm: Fox Trot

Words and Music by Kim Gannon
and Walter Kent

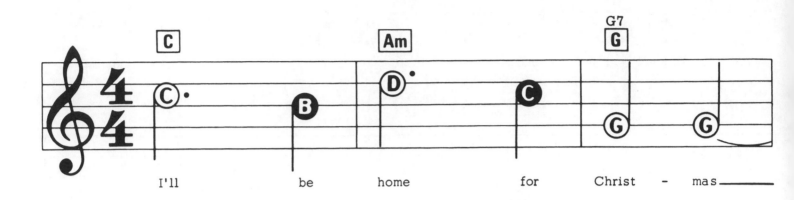

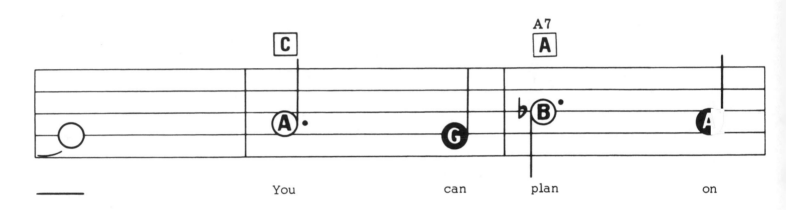

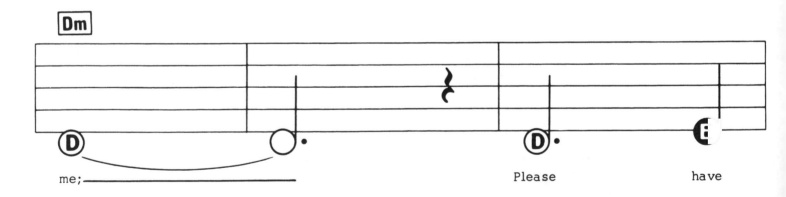

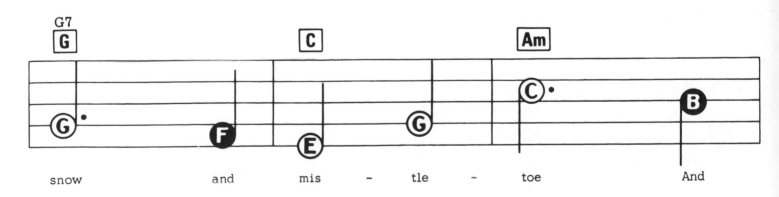

39

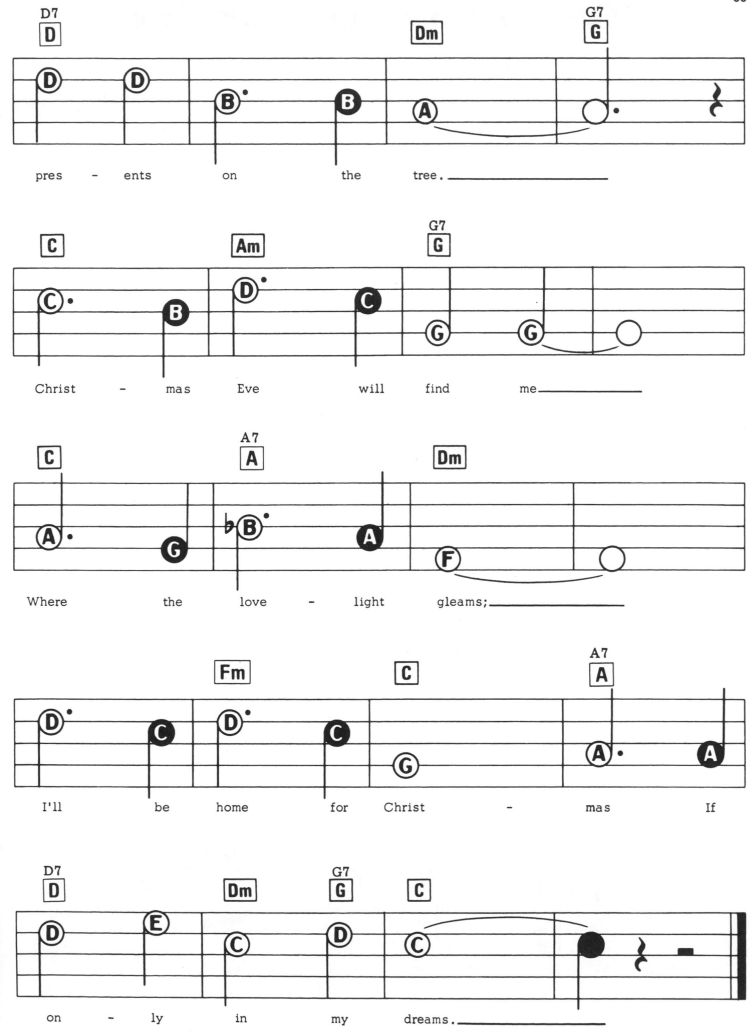

The Little Drummer Boy

Registration 2
Rhythm: March

Words and Music by Harry Simeone,
Henry Onorati and Katherine Davis

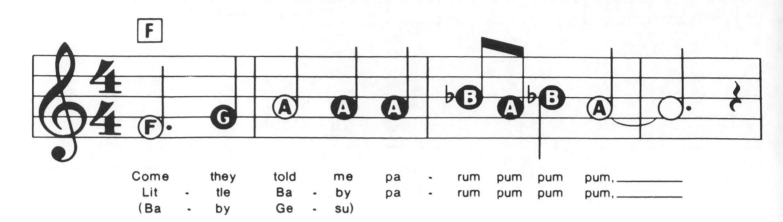

Come they told me pa - rum pum pum pum, _____
Lit - tle Ba - by pa - rum pum pum pum, _____
(Ba - by Ge - su)

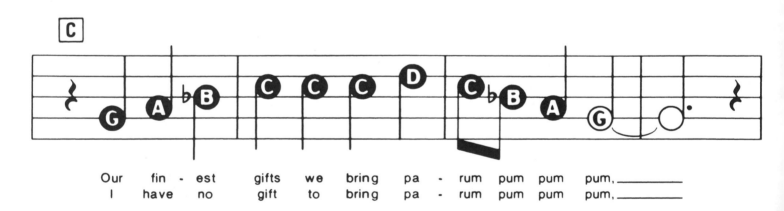

A new born King to see, pa - rum pum pum pum, _____
I am a poor boy too, pa - rum pum pum pum, _____

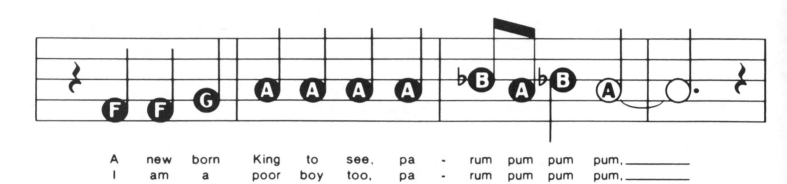

Our fin - est gifts we bring pa - rum pum pum pum, _____
I have no gift to bring pa - rum pum pum pum, _____

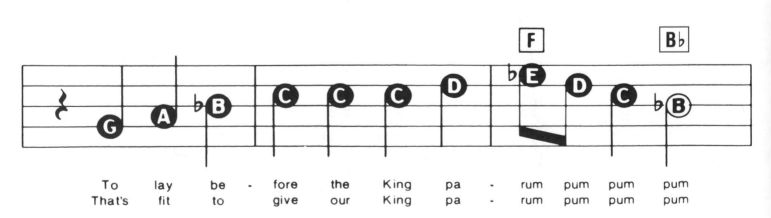

To lay be - fore the King pa - rum pum pum pum
That's fit to give our King pa - rum pum pum pum

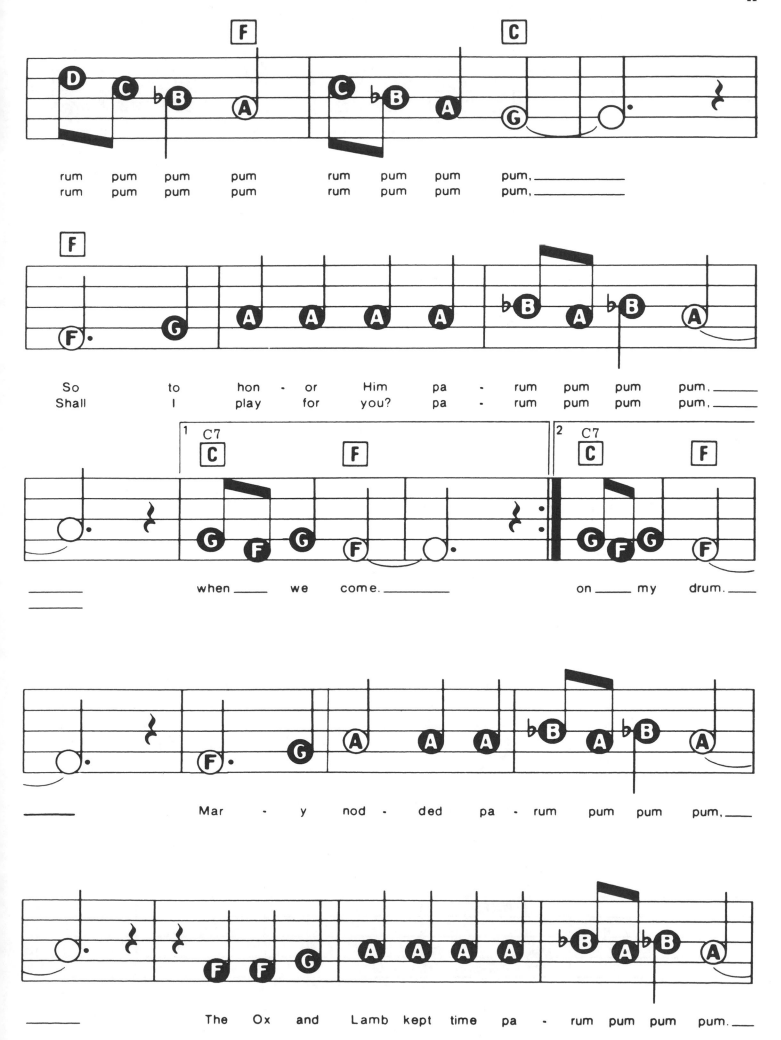

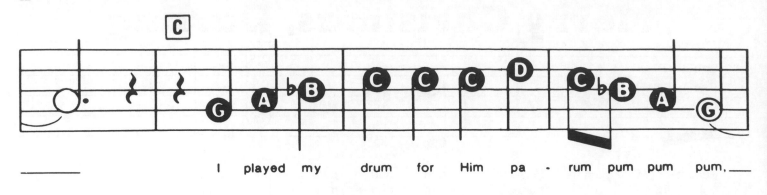

I played my drum for Him pa - rum pum pum pum,

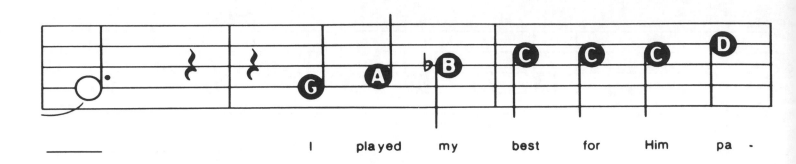

I played my best for Him pa -

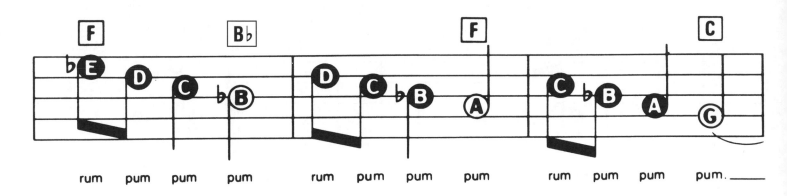

rum pum pum pum rum pum pum pum rum pum pum pum.

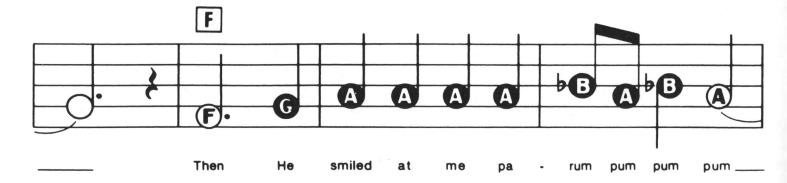

Then He smiled at me pa - rum pum pum pum

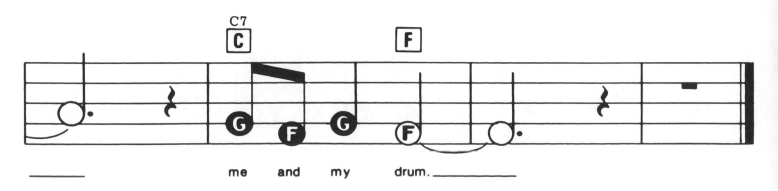

me and my drum.

Merry Christmas, Darling

Registration 1
Rhythm: Ballad

Words and Music by Richard Carpenter
and Frank Pooler

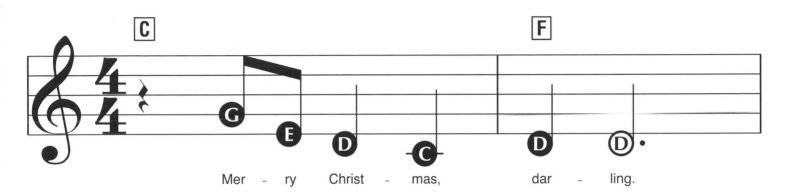

Mer - ry Christ - mas, dar - ling.

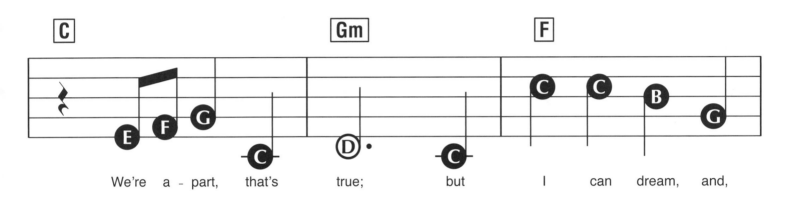

We're a - part, that's true; but I can dream, and,

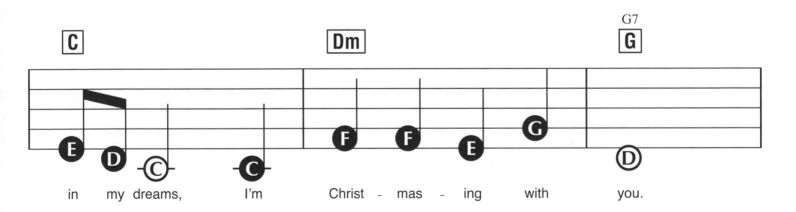

in my dreams, I'm Christ - mas - ing with you.

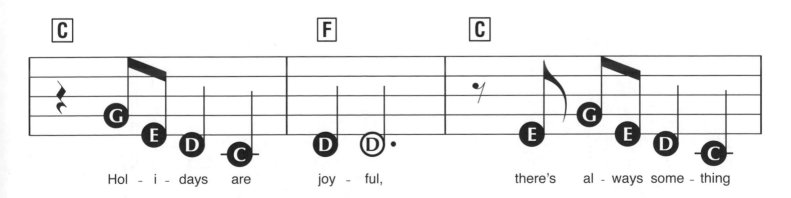

Hol - i - days are joy - ful, there's al - ways some - thing

44

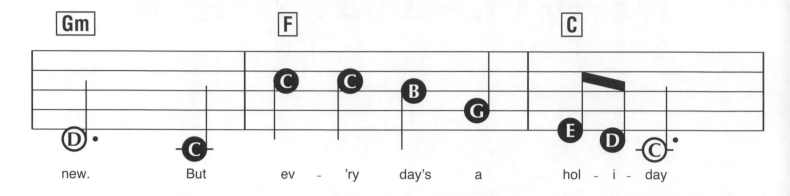

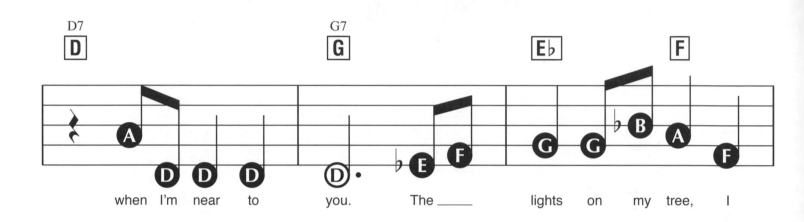

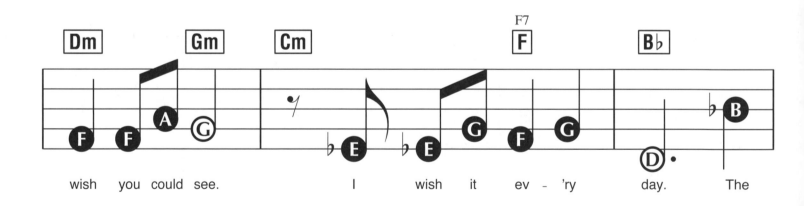

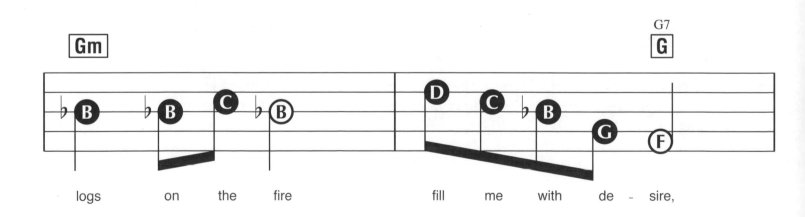

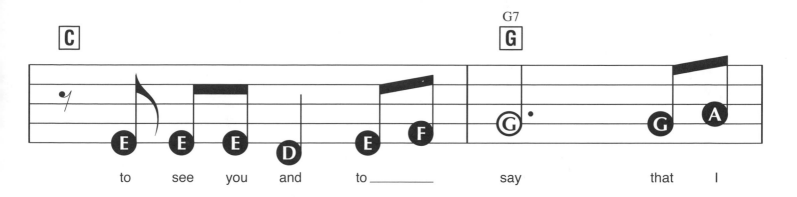

to see you and to _____ say that I

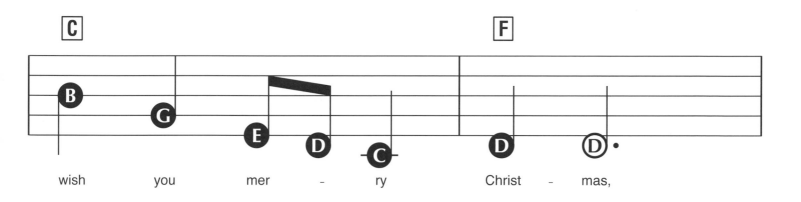

wish you mer - ry Christ - mas,

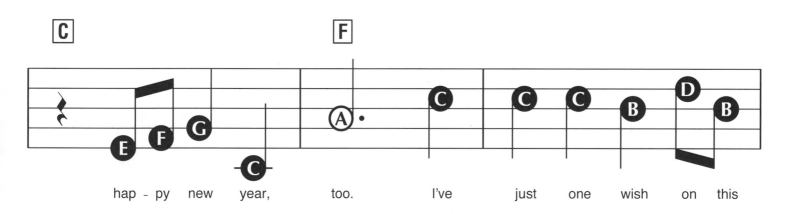

hap - py new year, too. I've just one wish on this

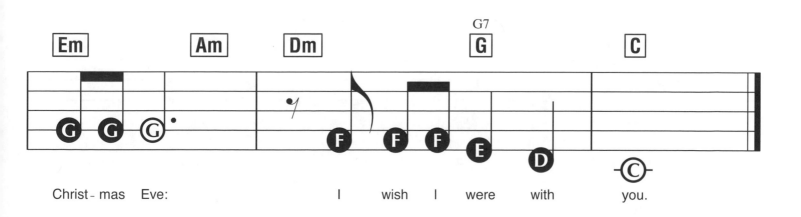

Christ - mas Eve: I wish I were with you.

Mary, Did You Know?

Registration 8
Rhythm: Ballad

Words and Music by Mark Lowry
and Buddy Greene

N.C. % **Dm**

D E F G   A D A

Mar - y, did you know that your
know that your
know that your

C **Gm**

G F E C   D E F G

ba - by boy _____ would one day walk _____ on
ba - by boy _____ will give sight to _____ a
ba - by boy _____ is Lord of all _____ cre -

A **Dm**

F E D E F G   A D A

wa - ter? Mar - y, did you know that your
blind man? Mar - y, did you know that your
a - tion? Mar - y, did you know that your

C **Gm**

G F E C   D E F G

ba - by boy _____ would save our sons _____ and
ba - by boy _____ would calm a storm _____ with
ba - by boy _____ will one day rule _____ the

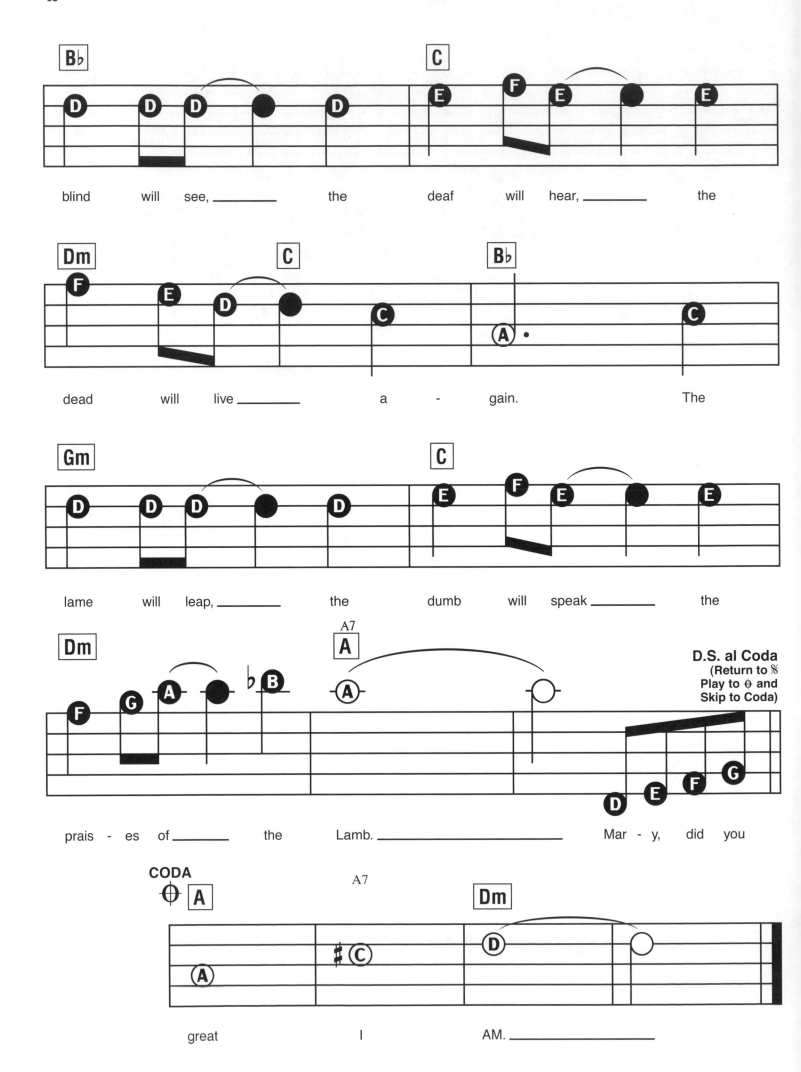

O Little Town of Bethlehem

Registration 1
Rhythm: Ballad or None

Words by Phillips Brooks
Music by Lewis H. Redner

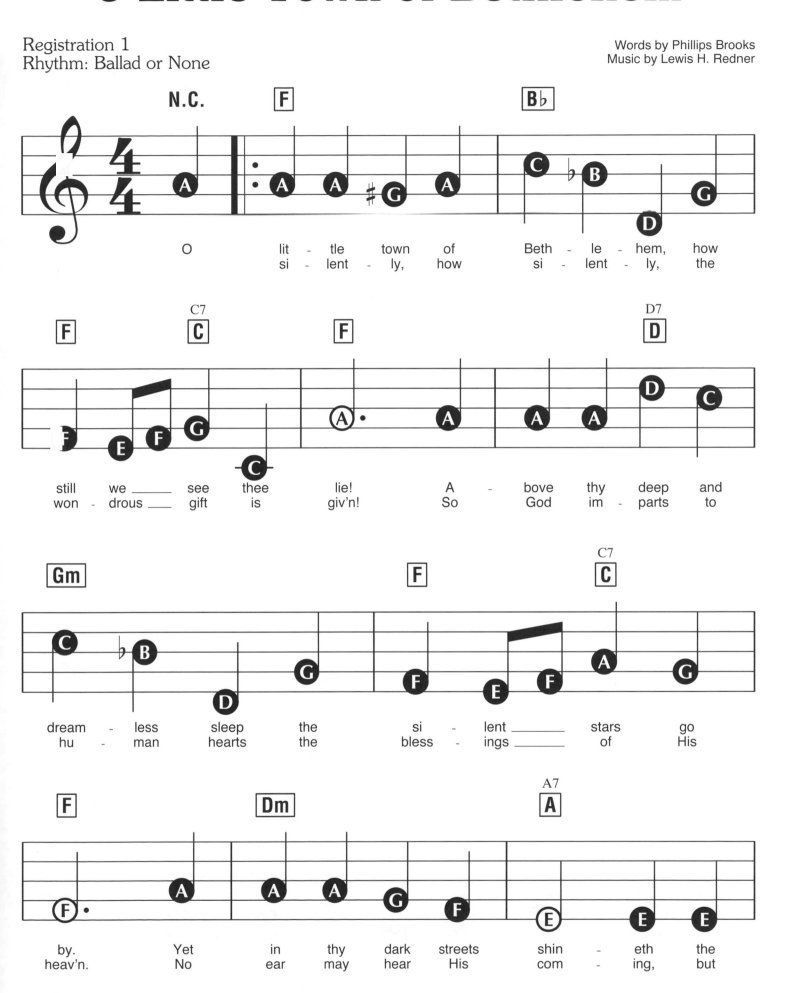

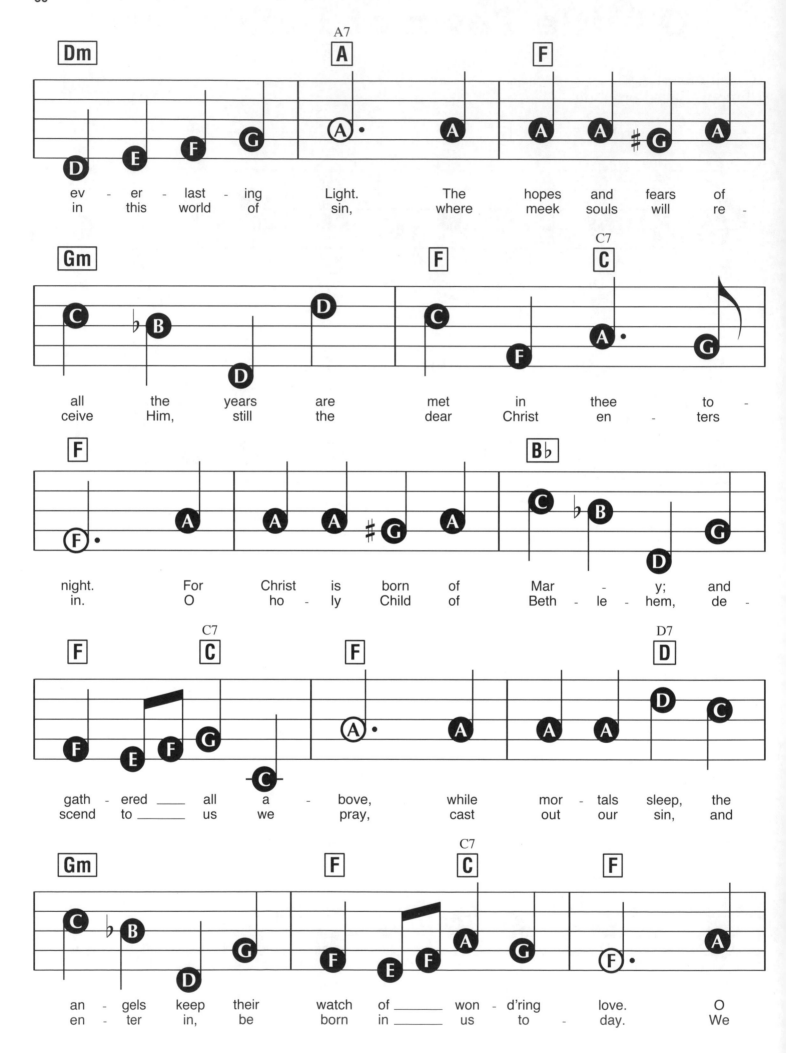

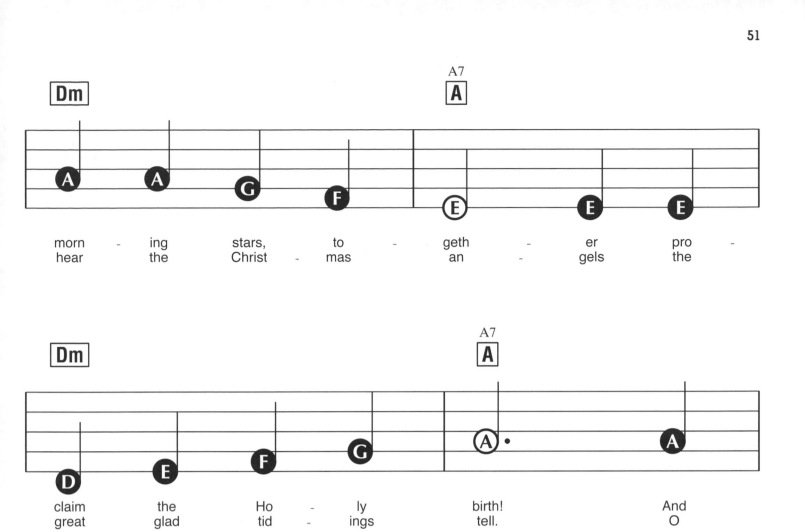

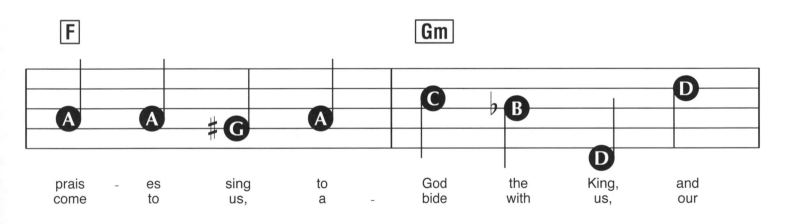

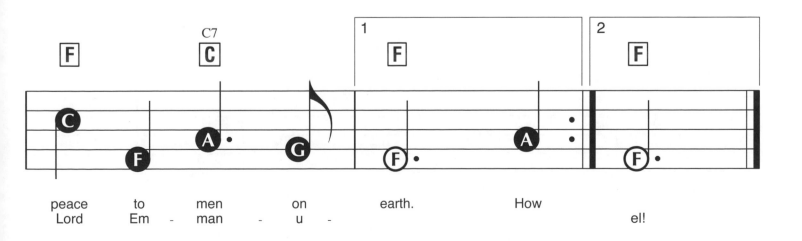

51

Mistletoe and Holly

Registration 2
Rhythm: Swing

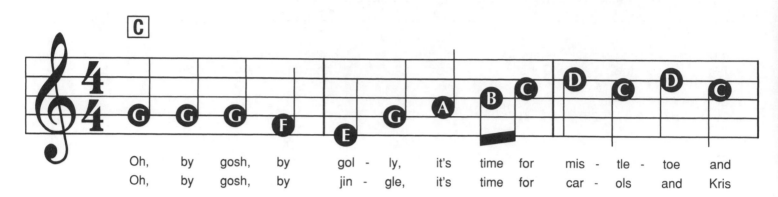

Words and Music by Frank Sinatra,
Dok Stanford and Henry W. Sanicola

Oh, by gosh, by gol - ly, it's time for mis - tle - toe and
Oh, by gosh, by jin - gle, it's time for car - ols and Kris

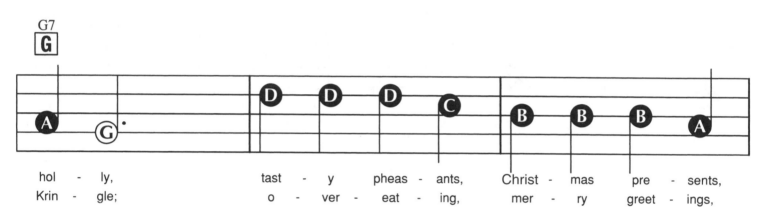

hol - ly, tast - y pheas - ants, Christ - mas pre - sents,
Krin - gle; o - ver - eat - ing, mer - ry greet - ings,

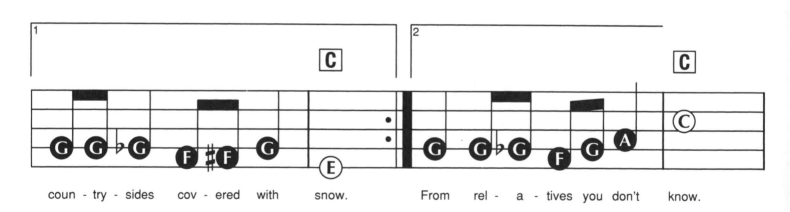

coun - try - sides cov - ered with snow.   From rel - a - tives you don't know.

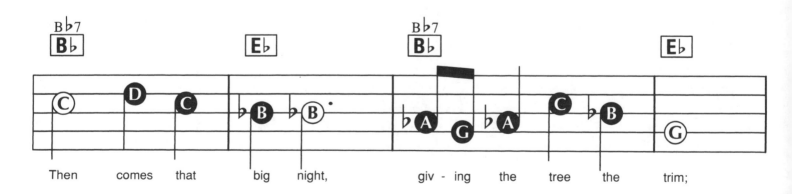

Then comes that big night, giv - ing the tree the trim;

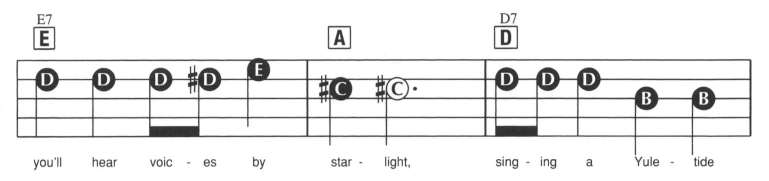

you'll hear voic - es by star - light, sing - ing a Yule - tide

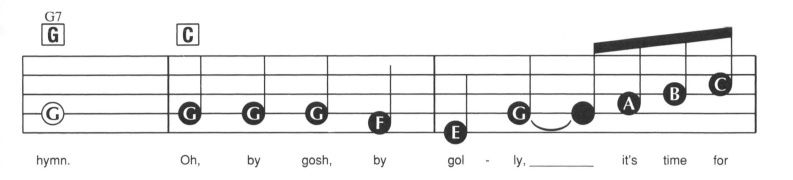

hymn. Oh, by gosh, by gol - ly, _____ it's time for

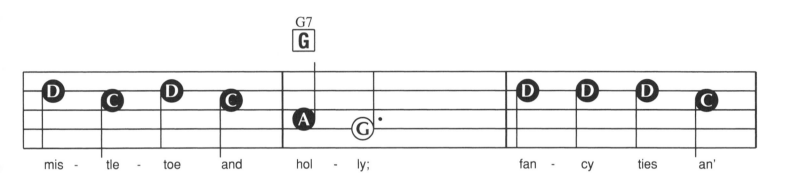

mis - tle - toe and hol - ly; fan - cy ties an'

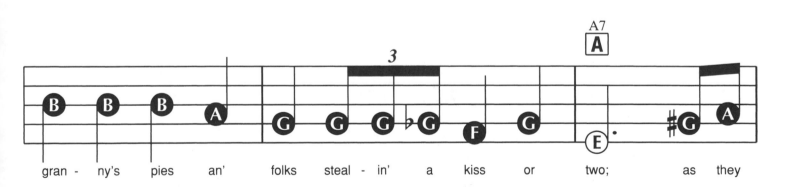

gran - ny's pies an' folks steal - in' a kiss or two; as they

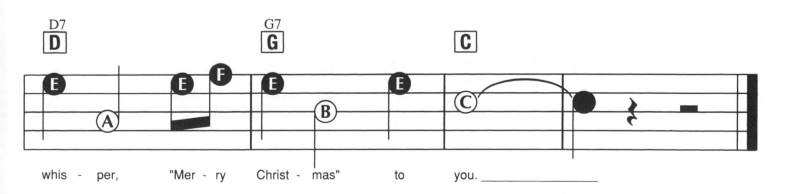

whis - per, "Mer - ry Christ - mas" to you. _____

The Most Wonderful Time of the Year

Registration 4
Rhythm: Jazz Waltz or Waltz

Words and Music by Eddie Pola
and George Wyle

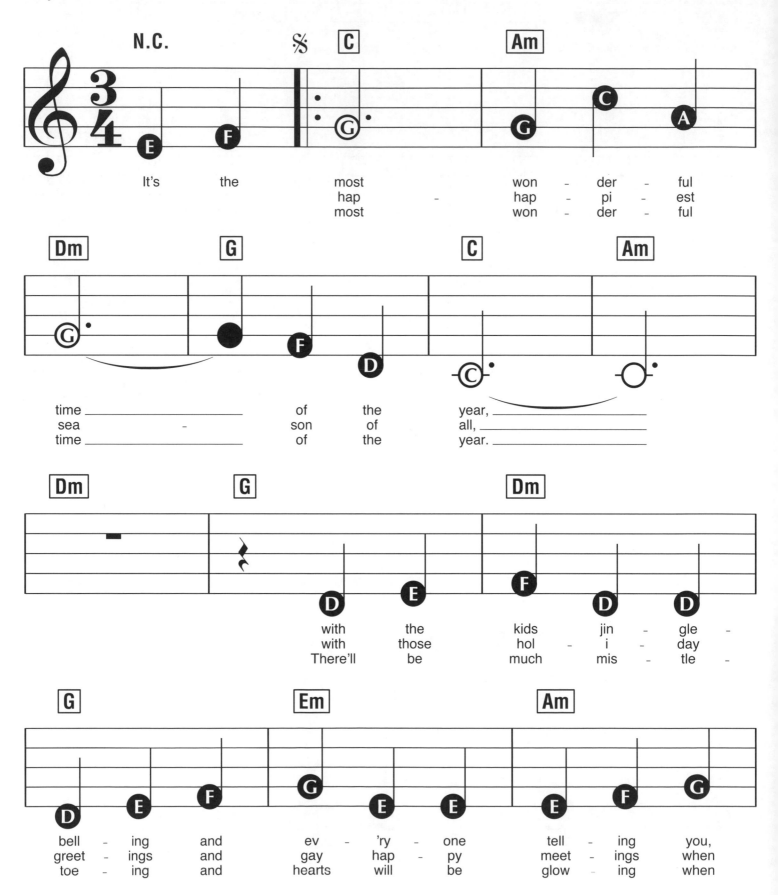

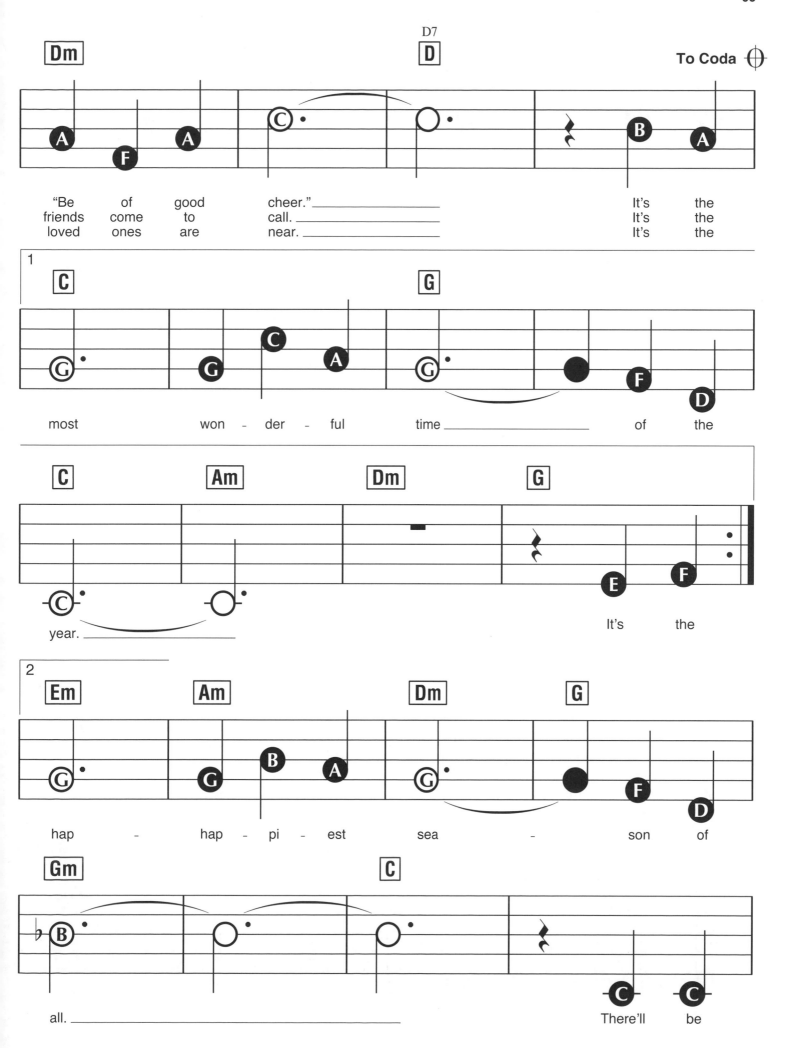

56

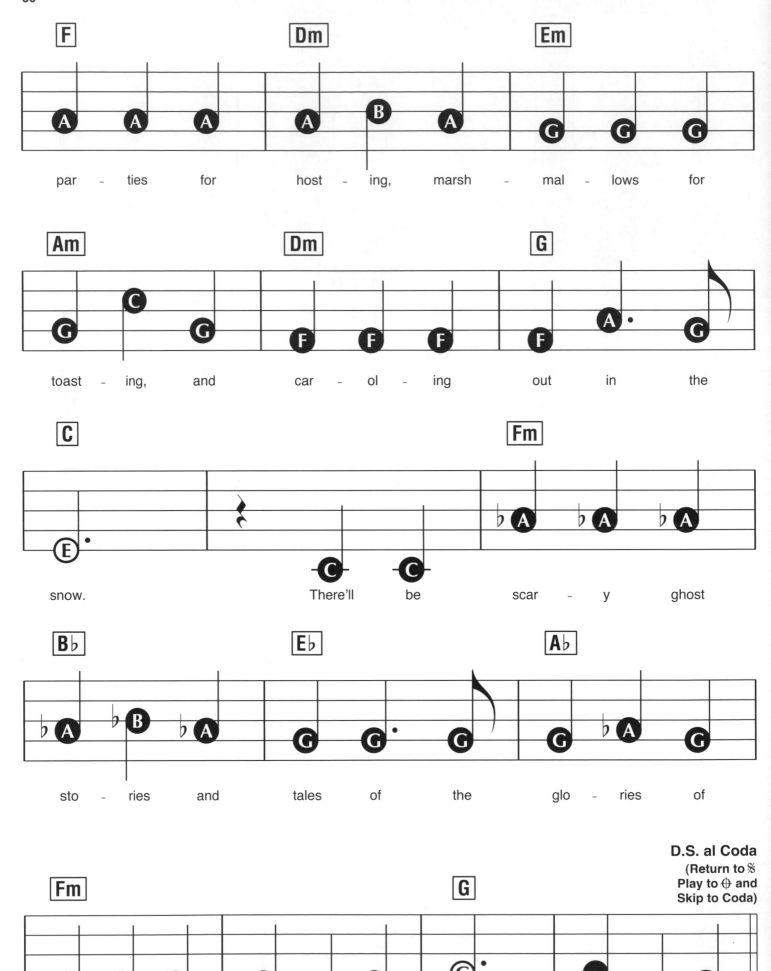

D.S. al Coda
(Return to 𝄋
Play to ⊕ and
Skip to Coda)

CODA

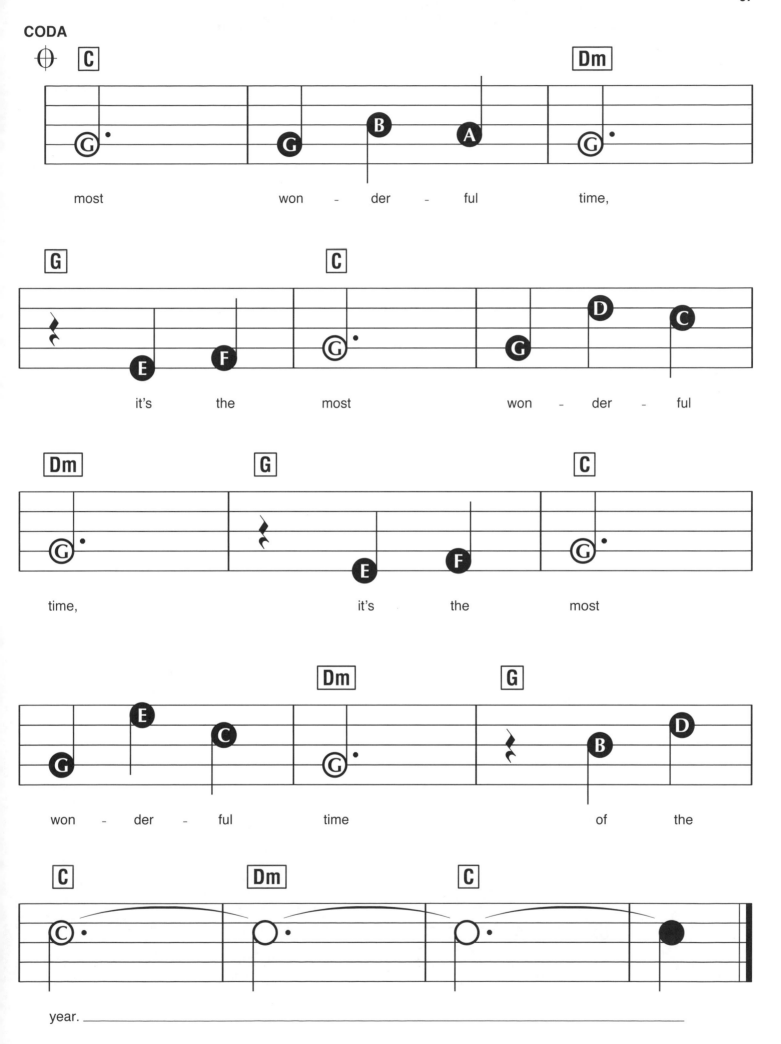

O Come, All Ye Faithful

Registration 6
Rhythm: None

Words and Music by
John Francis Wade
Latin Words translated by Frederick Oakeley

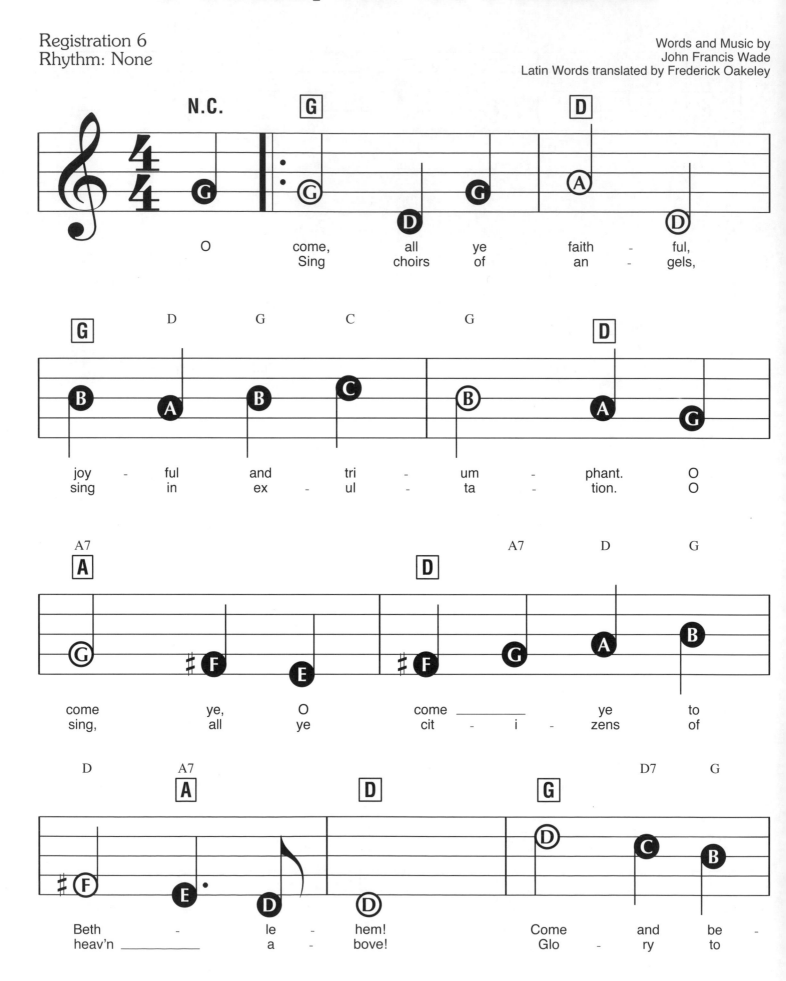

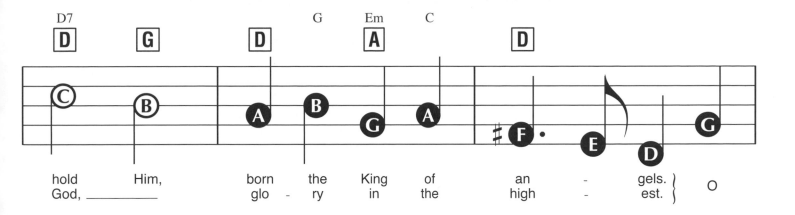

hold Him, born the King of the an - gels. ⎱
God, _____ glo - ry in of the high - est. ⎰ O

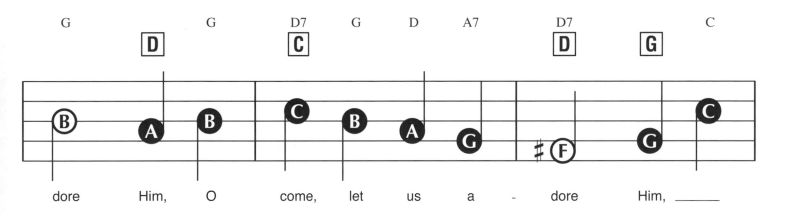

come, let us a - dore Him, O come, let us a -

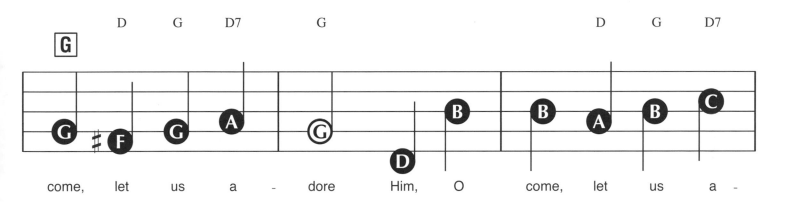

dore Him, O come, let us a - dore Him, _____

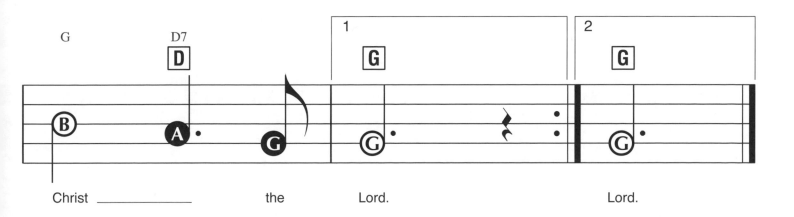

Christ _____ the Lord. Lord.

Rockin' Around the Christmas Tree

Registration 2
Rhythm: Swing

Music and Lyrics by
Johnny Marks

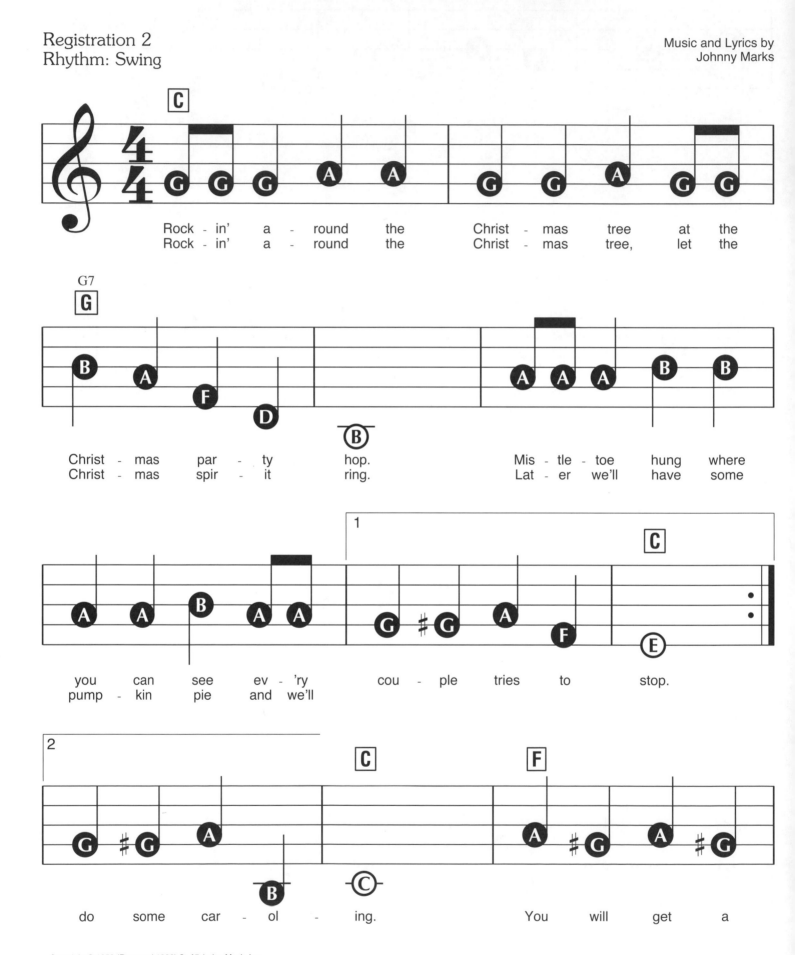

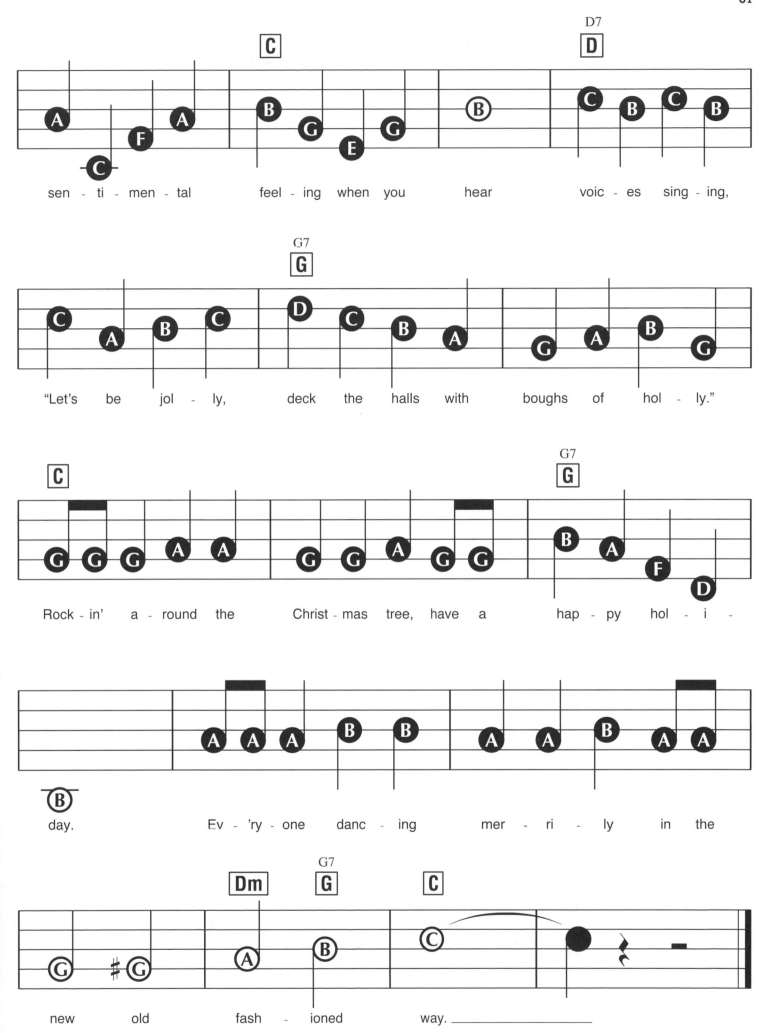

Rudolph the Red-Nosed Reindeer

Registration 4
Rhythm: Fox Trot or Swing

Music and Lyrics by
Johnny Marks

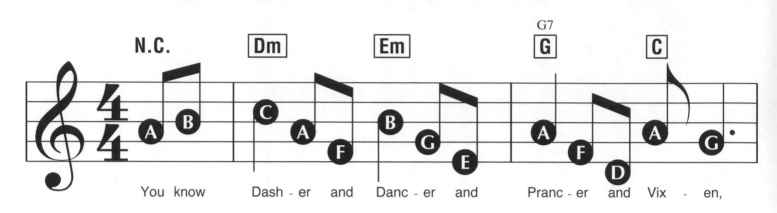

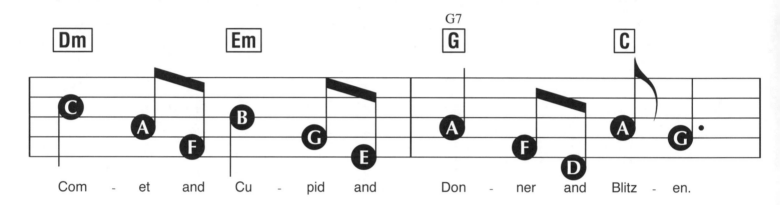

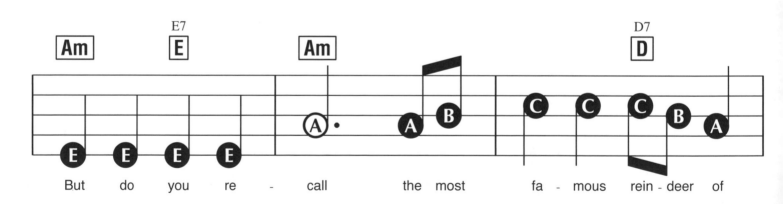

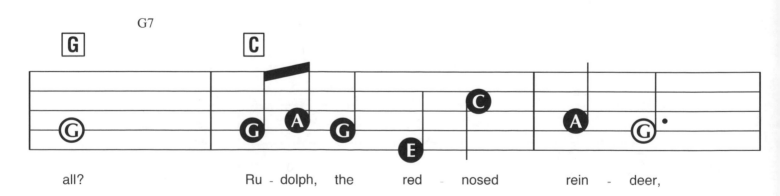

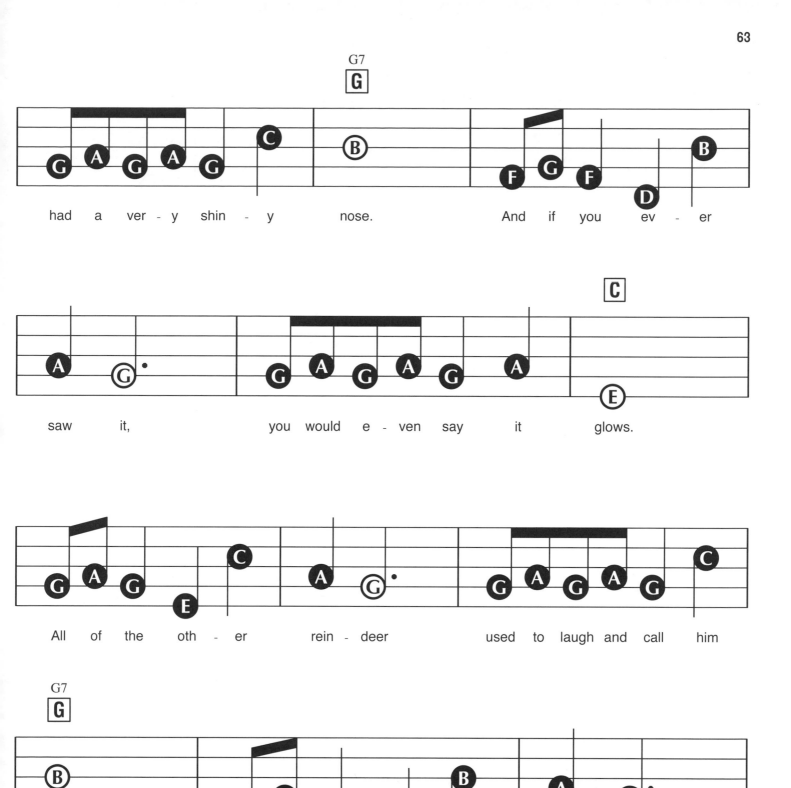

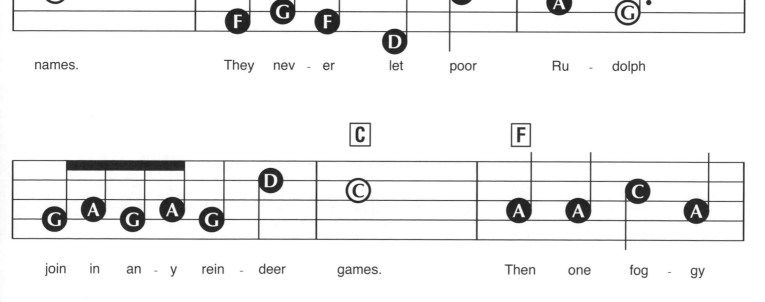

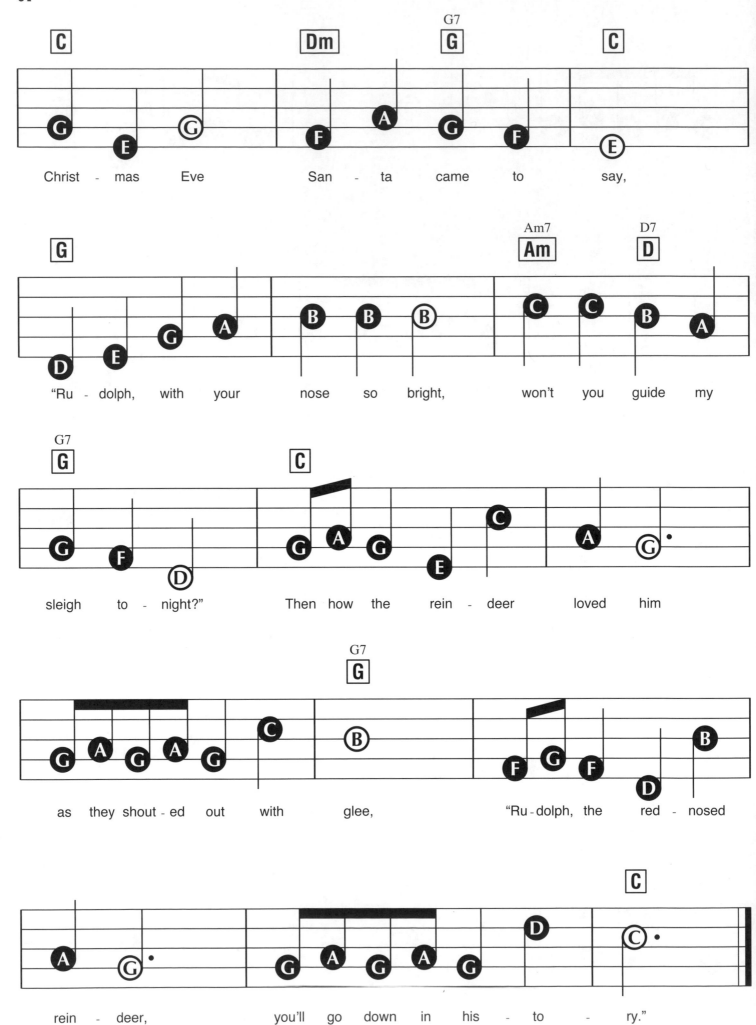

Silver Bells
from the Paramount Picture THE LEMON DROP KID

Registration 5
Rhythm: Waltz

Words and Music by Jay Livingston
and Ray Evans

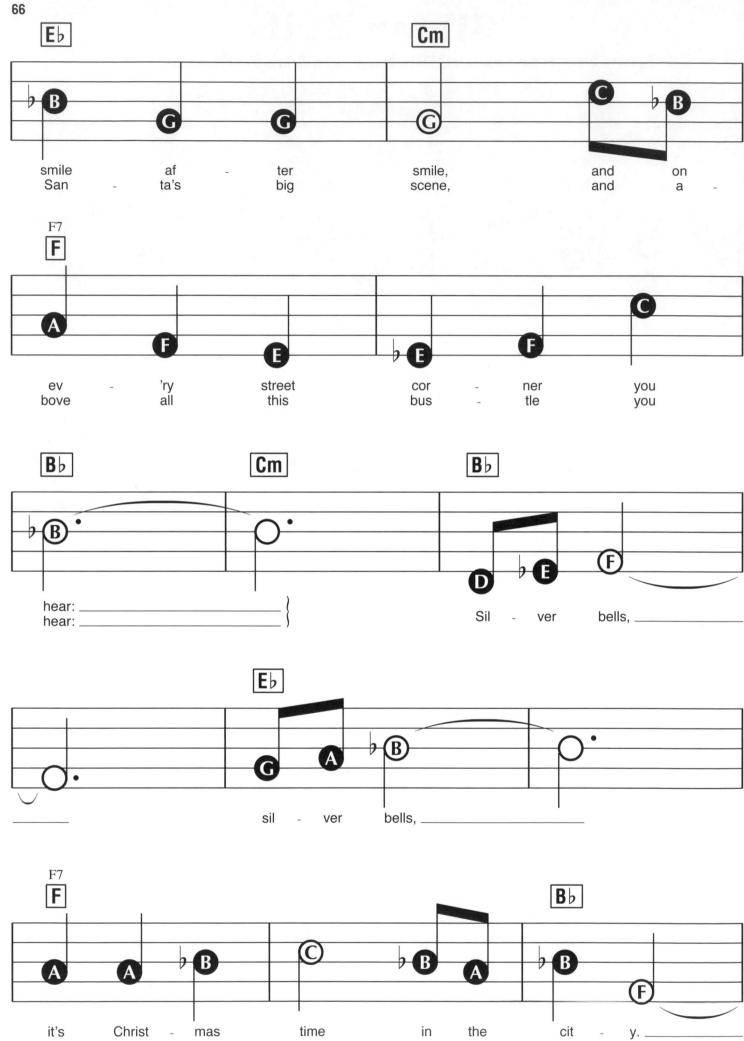

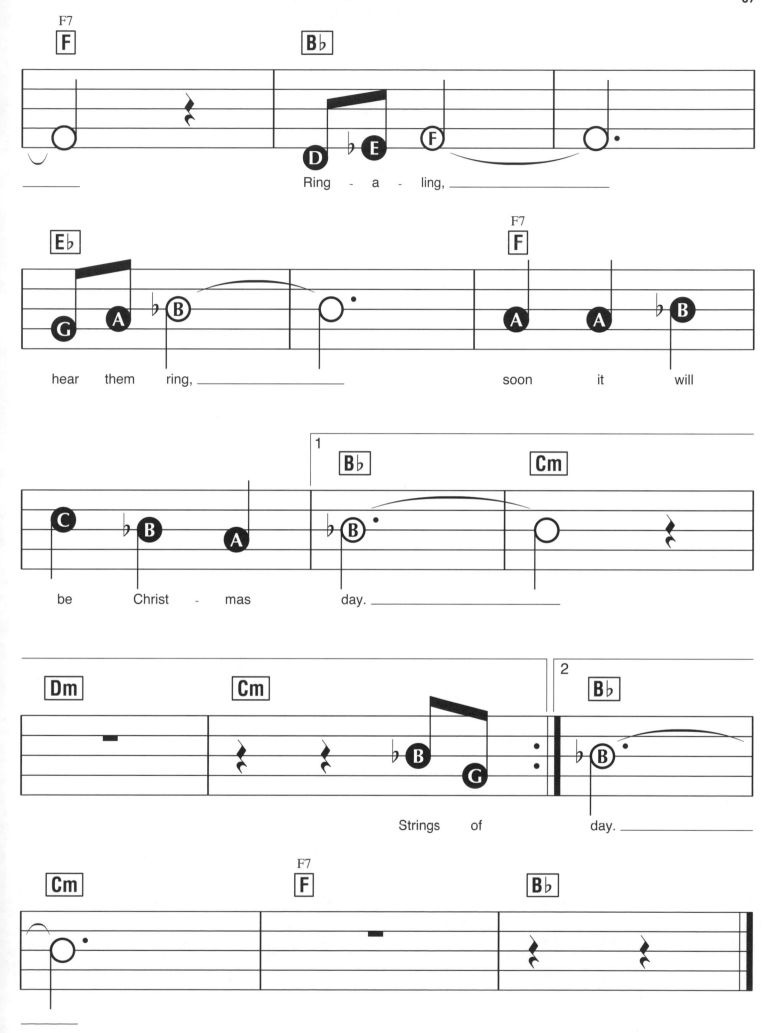

Silent Night

Registration 1
Rhythm: Waltz

Words by Joseph Mohr
Translated by John F. Young
Music by Franz X. Grüber

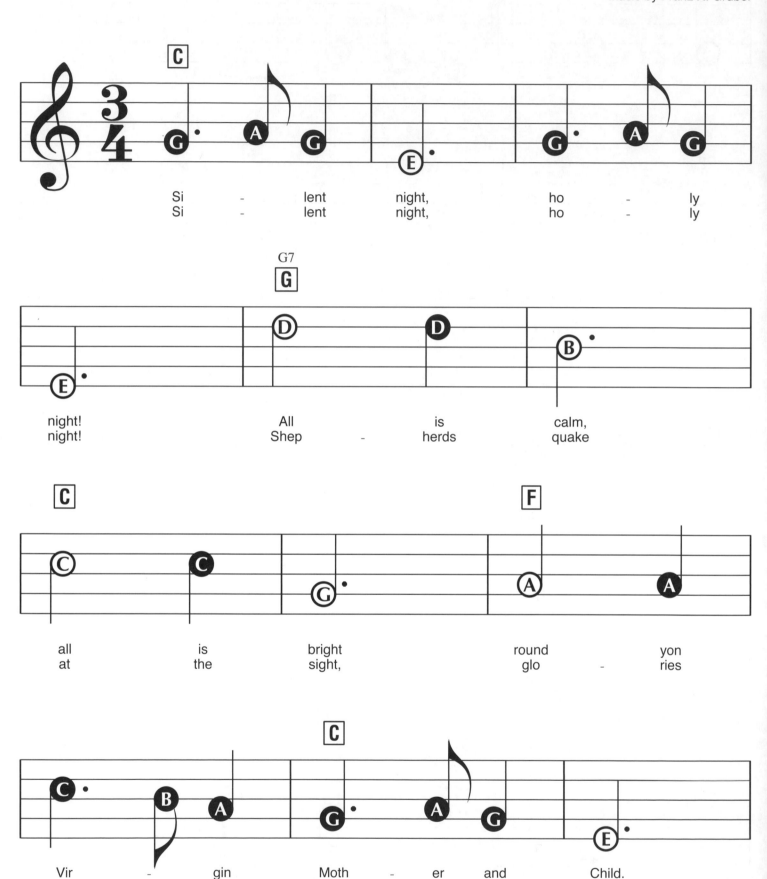

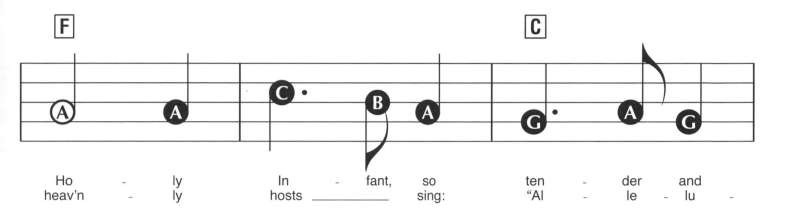

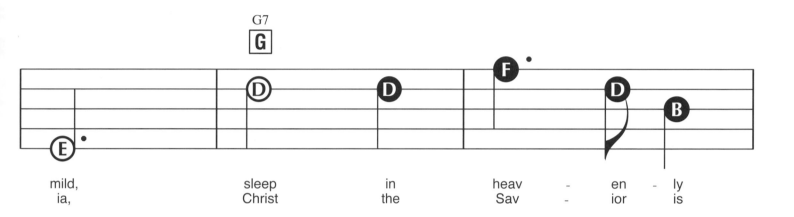

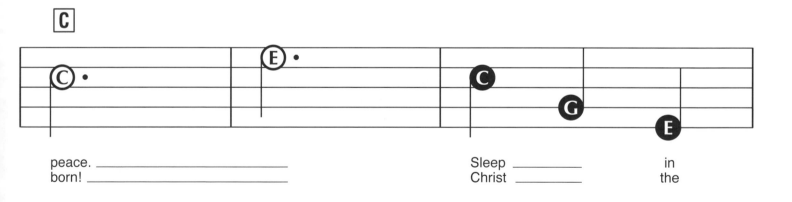

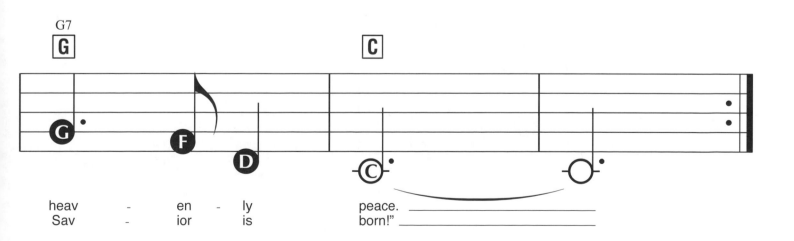

Sleigh Ride

Registration 5
Rhythm: Fox Trot

Music by Leroy Anderson
Words by Mitchell Parish

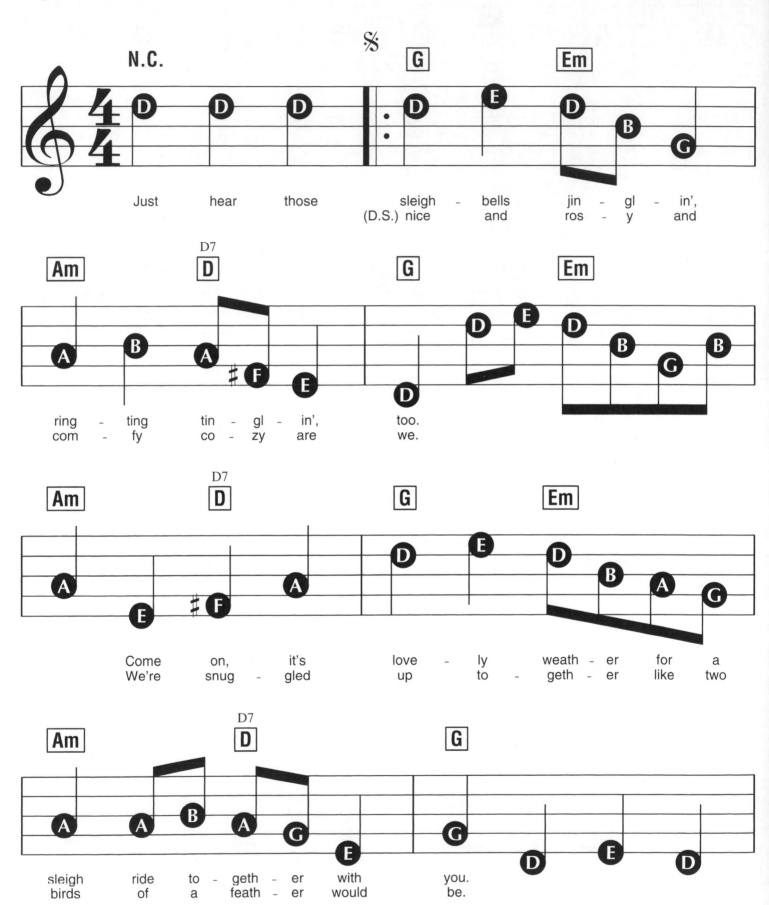

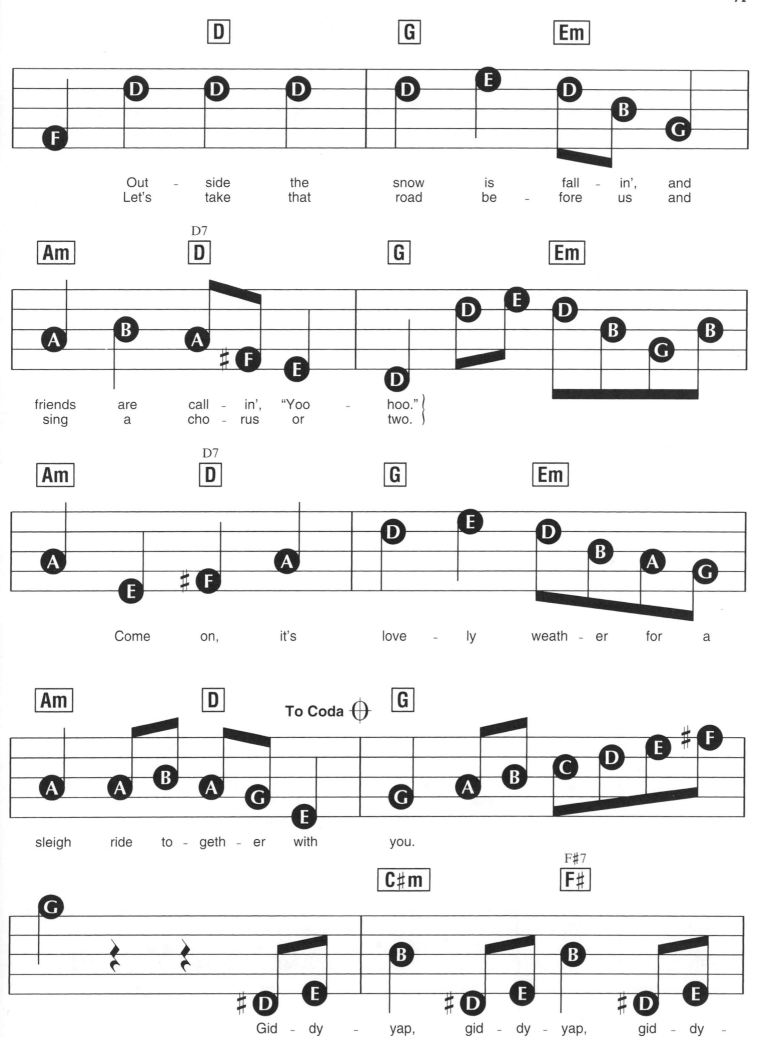

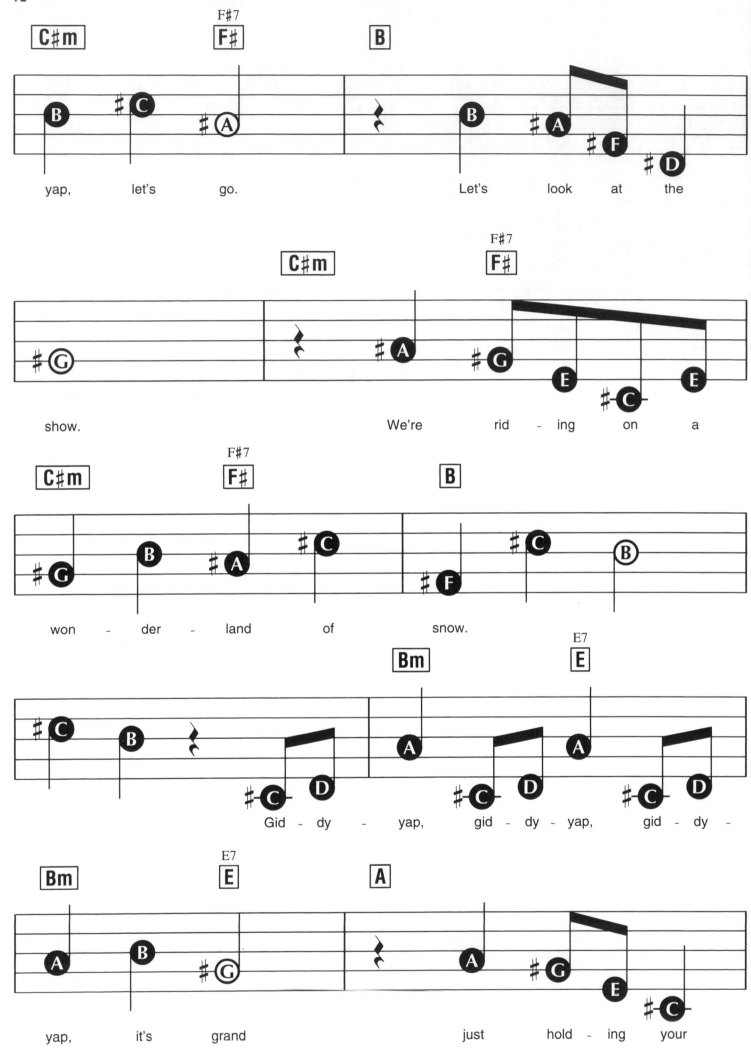

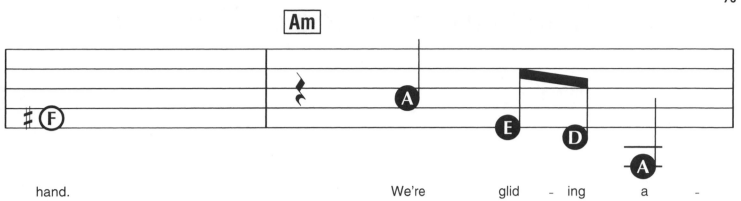

hand.   We're   glid - ing   a -

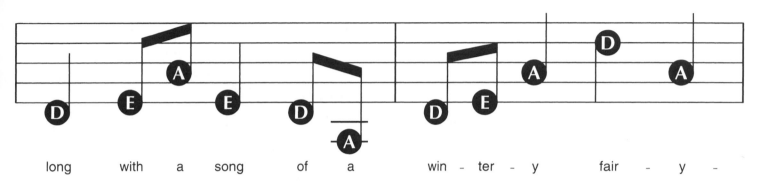

long   with   a   song   of   a   win - ter - y   fair - y -

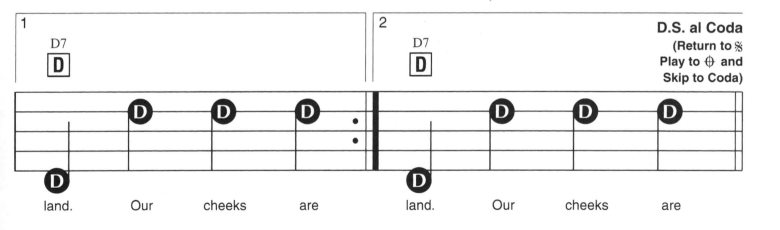

1
D7
land.   Our   cheeks   are

2
D7
land.   Our   cheeks   are

D.S. al Coda
(Return to ℅
Play to ⊕ and
Skip to Coda)

CODA
⊕

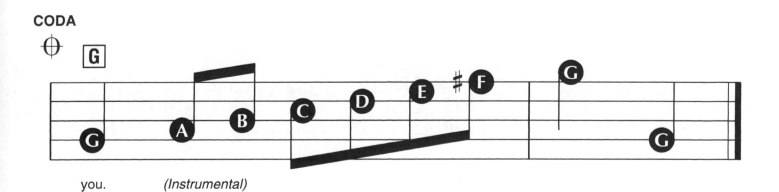

you.   *(Instrumental)*

The Twelve Days of Christmas

Registration 5
Rhythm: None

Traditional English Carol

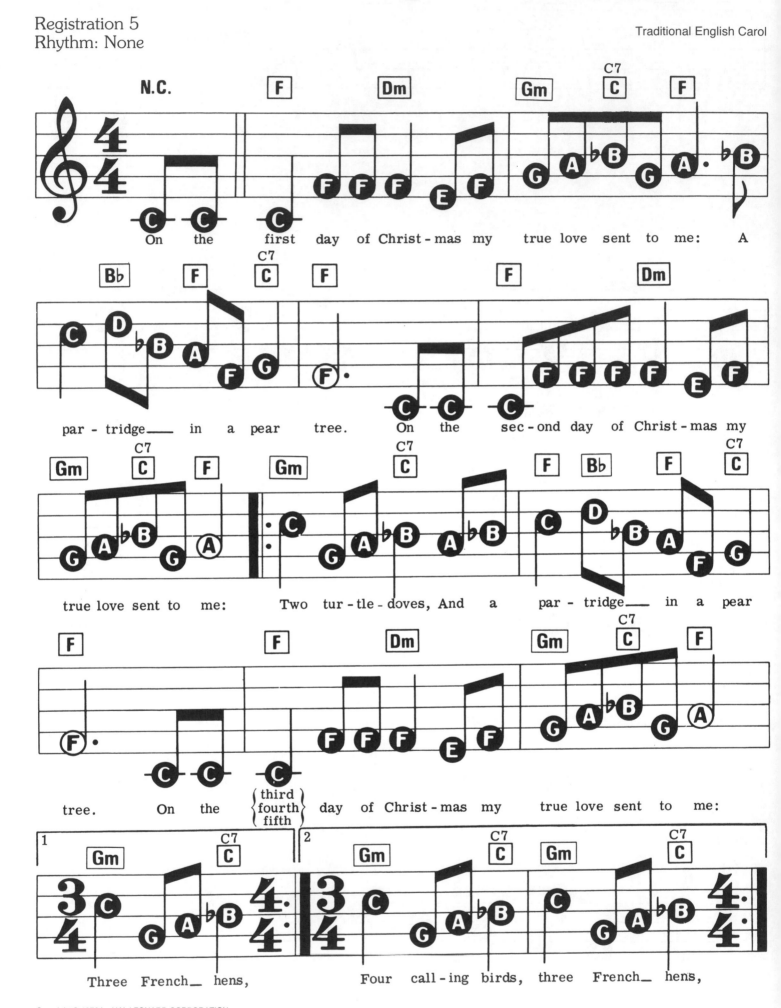

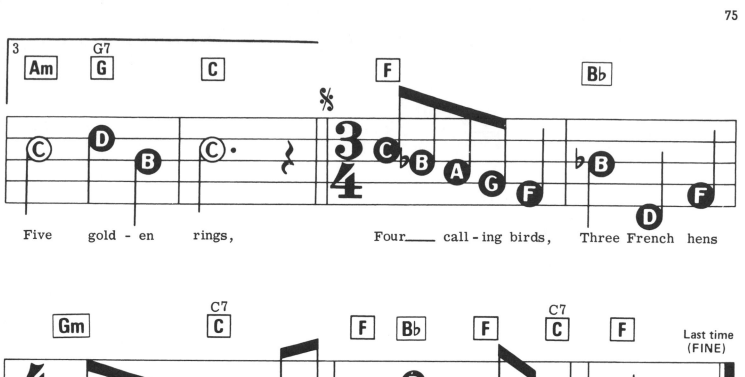

Five gold - en rings, Four___ call - ing birds, Three French hens

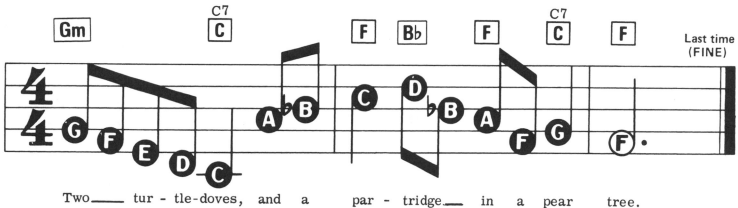

Two___ tur - tle - doves, and a par - tridge___ in a pear tree.

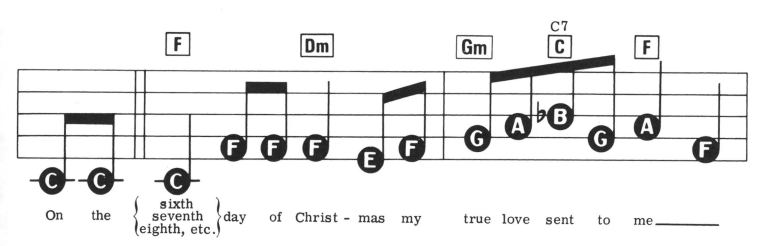

On the { sixth seventh eighth, etc. } day of Christ - mas my true love sent to me___

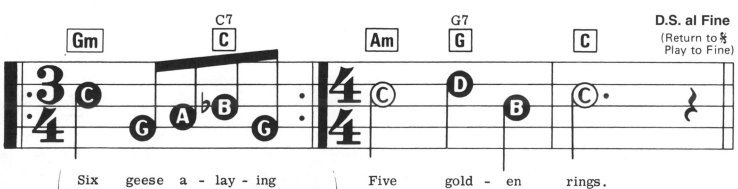

D.S. al Fine
(Return to %
Play to Fine)

Six geese a - lay - ing
Seven swans a - swim-ming (to 6)
Eight maids a - milk - ing (to 7)
Nine la - dies danc - ing (to 8)
Ten lords a - leap - ing (to 9)
Eleven pi - pers pip - ing (to 10)
Twelve drum-mers drum-ming (to 11)

Five gold - en rings.

We Wish You a Merry Christmas

Registration 7
Rhythm: Waltz

Traditional English Folksong

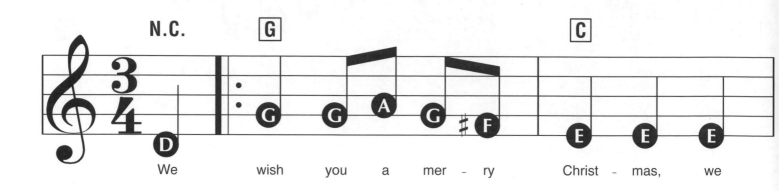

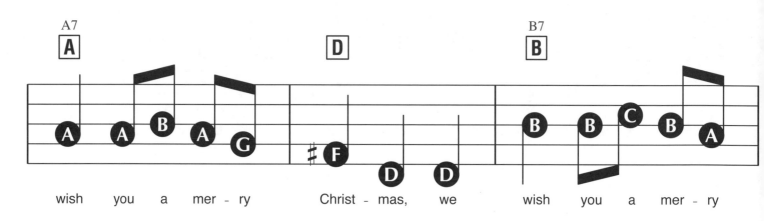

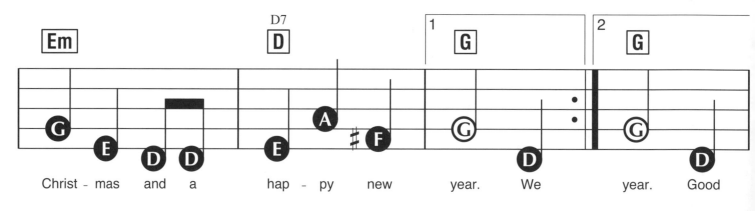

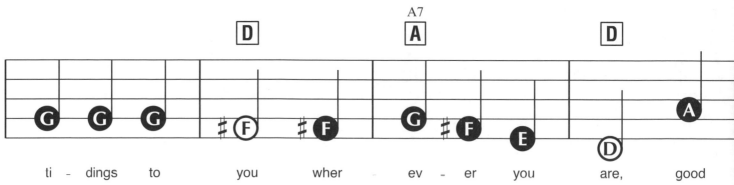

(Instrumental)

What Are You Doing New Year's Eve?

Registration 3
Rhythm: Fox Trot or Swing

By Frank Loesser

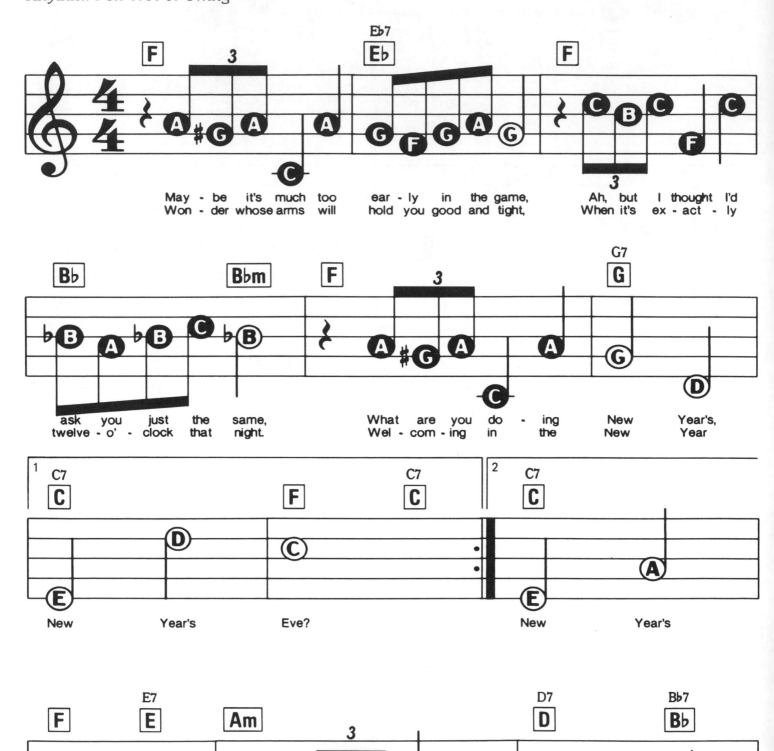

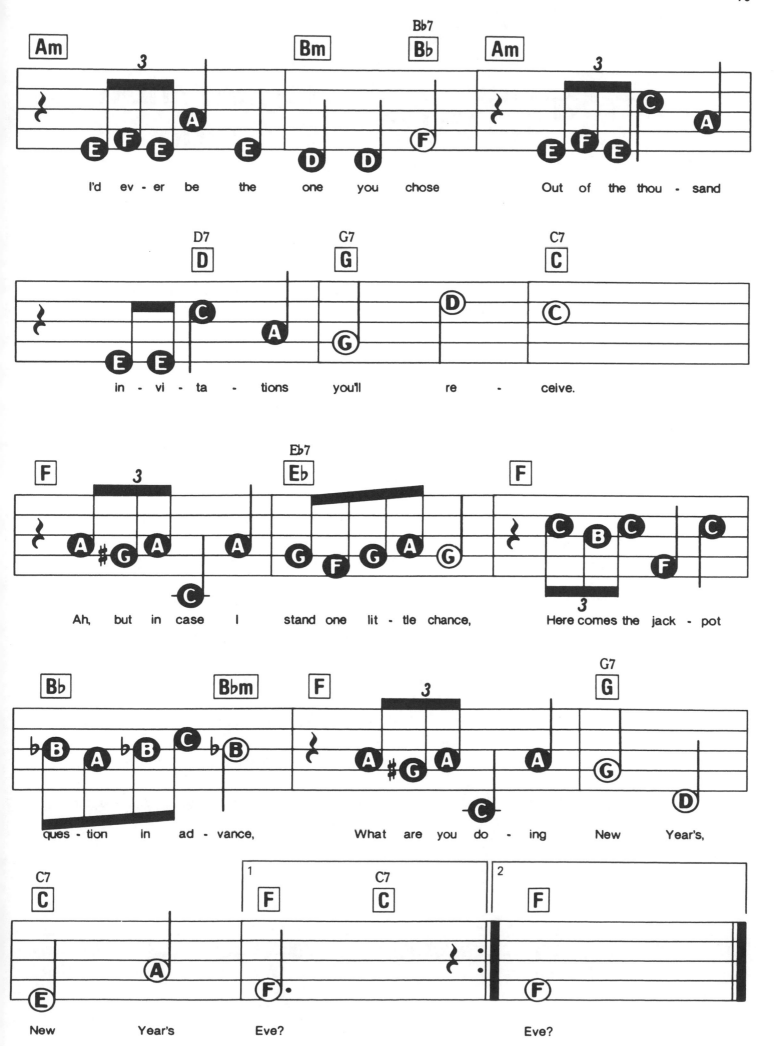

Registration Guide

- Match the Registration number on the song to the corresponding numbered category below. Select and activate an instrumental sound available on your instrument.

- Choose an automatic rhythm appropriate to the mood and style of the song. (Consult your Owner's Guide for proper operation of automatic rhythm features.)

- Adjust the tempo and volume controls to comfortable settings.

Registration

1	Mellow	Flutes, Clarinet, Oboe, Flugel Horn, Trombone, French Horn, Organ Flutes
2	Ensemble	Brass Section, Sax Section, Wind Ensemble, Full Organ, Theater Organ
3	Strings	Violin, Viola, Cello, Fiddle, String Ensemble, Pizzicato, Organ Strings
4	Guitars	Acoustic/Electric Guitars, Banjo, Mandolin, Dulcimer, Ukulele, Hawaiian Guitar
5	Mallets	Vibraphone, Marimba, Xylophone, Steel Drums, Bells, Celesta, Chimes
6	Liturgical	Pipe Organ, Hand Bells, Vocal Ensemble, Choir, Organ Flutes
7	Bright	Saxophones, Trumpet, Mute Trumpet, Synth Leads, Jazz/Gospel Organs
8	Piano	Piano, Electric Piano, Honky Tonk Piano, Harpsichord, Clavi
9	Novelty	Melodic Percussion, Wah Trumpet, Synth, Whistle, Kazoo, Perc. Organ
10	Bellows	Accordion, French Accordion, Mussette, Harmonica, Pump Organ, Bagpipes